PELIC

THE DEAD

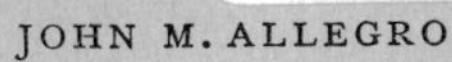

JOHN M. ALLEGRO

The Dead Sea Scrolls

JOHN M. ALLEGRO

PENGUIN BOOKS

Penguin Books Ltd, Harmondsworth, Middlesex
U.S.A.: Penguin Books Inc., 3300 Clipper Mill Road, Baltimore 11, Md
CANADA: Penguin Books (Canada) Ltd, 178 Norseman Street,
Toronto 18, Ontario
AUSTRALIA: Penguin Books Pty Ltd, 762 Whitehorse Road,
Mitcham, Victoria
SOUTH AFRICA : Penguin Books (S.A.) Pty Ltd, Gibraltar House,
Regent Road, Sea Point, Cape Town

—

First published 1956

Made and printed in Great Britain
by C. Nicholls & Company Ltd

FOR JOAN

CONTENTS

LIST OF PLATES

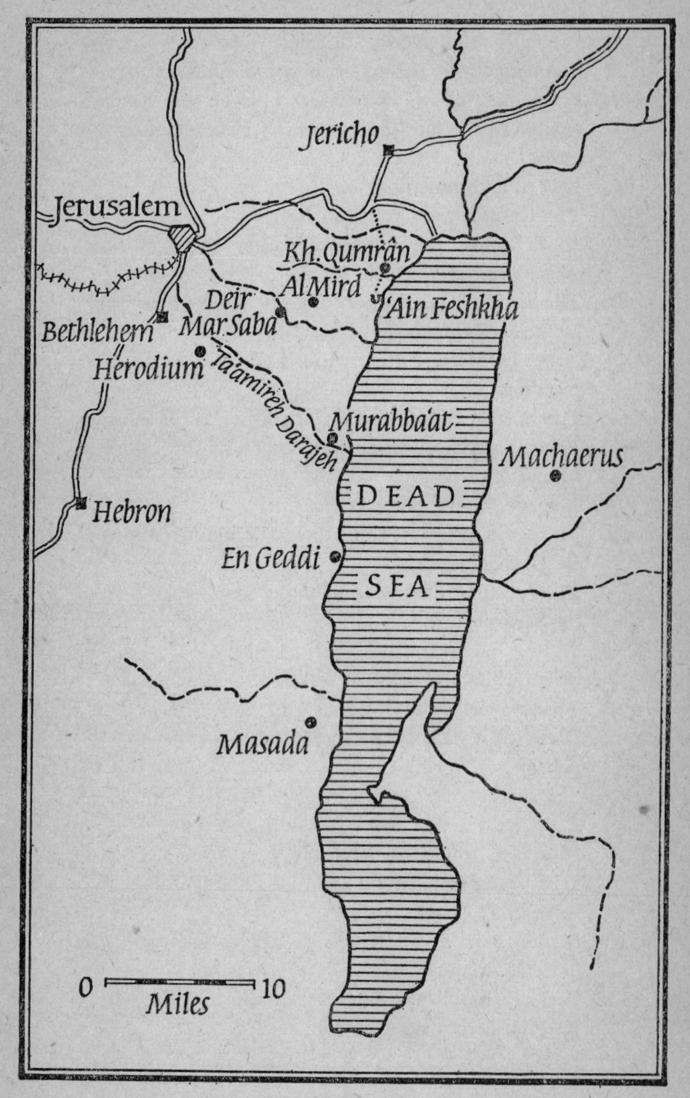
Jericho
Jerusalem
Kh. Qumrân
Al Mird
Deir
Mar Saba
'Ain Feshkha
Bethlehem
Herodium
Ta'âmireh
Darajeh
Murabba'at
Machaerus
DEAD
SEA
Hebron
En Geddi
Masada
0
10
Miles

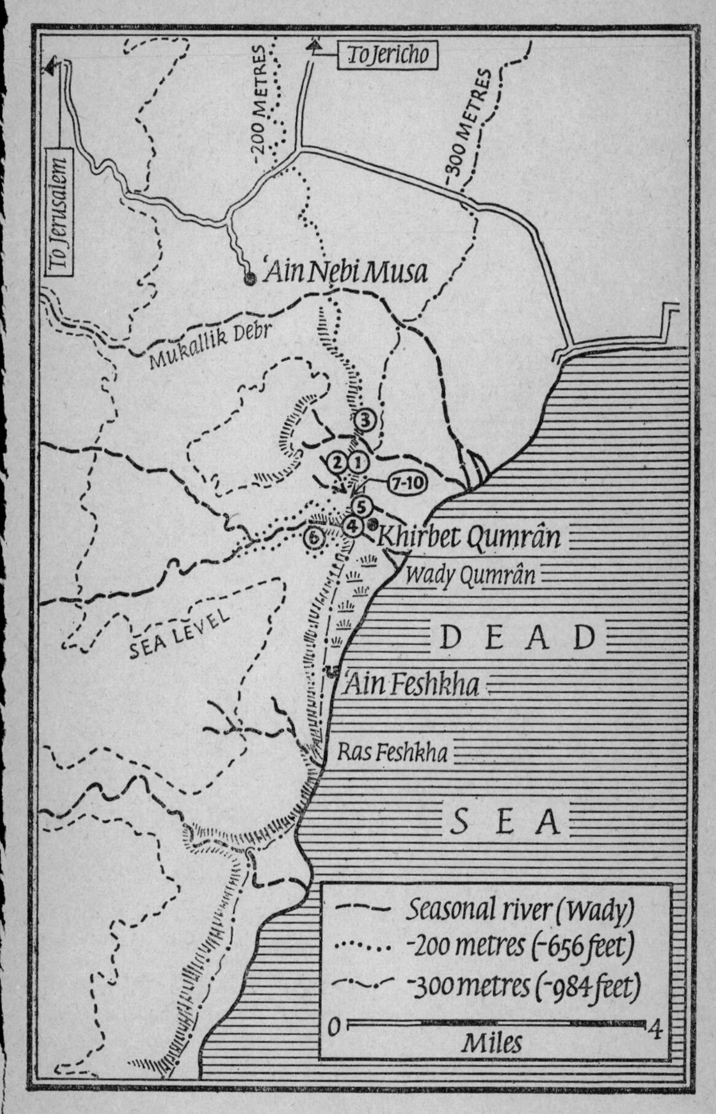
To Jericho
To Jerusalem
-200 METRES
300 METRES
'Ain Nebi Musa
Mukallik Debr
7-10
Khirbet Qumrân
Wady Qumrân
SEA LEVEL
D E A D
'Ain Feshkha
Ras Feshkha
S E A
Seasonal river (Wady)
-200 metres (-656 feet)
-300 metres (-984 feet)
0
4
Miles

PREFACE

The following chapters make no claim to being an exhaustive study of this fabulous documentary and archaeological material from the Dead Sea; such would be quite outside the scope of a small, popular volume. It does attempt to give to the general public some conception of the extent and importance of recent discoveries in this area, and I hope in a perspective made possible by a study of the published and unpublished material alike. If, as seems probable, this volume appears in print before the full publication of many of my documentary sources, let me apologize in advance for the irritation this may cause specialists in the field. They may rest assured that work in the Jerusalem 'Scrollery' is proceeding as fast as money and facilities become available for our journeys to Jordan. At least, we can feel glad that three years of begging has produced the money needed for the rescue of these precious scrolls, and work now on the assumption that most of what still survives is in our hands.

My debt to the vast amount of scholarship which has already gone into the study of the published scrolls will be self-evident to the specialist, and a perusal of the appended select bibliography will make the sources of many of the ideas used here immediately apparent. I should, however, like to pay a special tribute to the sterling pioneer work of Professor K. G. Kuhn in those aspects of the Scrolls affecting Christian origins.

Personal acknowledgements must begin with an expression of gratitude to Mr Gerald Lankester Harding and Father R. de Vaux, O.P., for their allowing me to take part in the editing of the Scroll fragments, and for valuable help and advice on the archaeological chapters. To Mr Joseph Saad, Secretary of the Palestine Archaeological Museum in Jerusalem, I am greatly indebted for much 'inside information' on the early stages of the tracing and purchase of the Scroll fragments, and to my colleagues in the 'Scrollery' for much kind advice, although it must be stated that responsibility for opinions expressed in these pages is entirely my own.

I should also like to thank the Matron and masters of St George's Upper School, Jerusalem, for their kind hospitality and invaluable discussion on these chapters, and also my friends at Hebron.

PREFACE

The Trustees of the Palestine Archaeological Museum have been most generous in the loan of copyright photographs for reproduction in these pages (plates 1, 6, 7, 12, 13, 20–4, 26, 30–5, 37, 39–42), as has Father L. H. Grollenberg in respect of plates 2, 4, 9, 25, 27–9, 38, and Father Jean Starcky for plates 16 and 36. Mr Harding on behalf of the Jordan Department of Antiquities kindly lent me plate 5.

I have been fortunate in having generous access to the characteristically complete Scrolls bibliography of Professor H. H. Rowley, and my wife has helped greatly by her clerical assistance in compiling my selection, as well as in proof-reading and many other necessary tasks involved in the production of this book.

CHAPTER ONE

THE DISCOVERY AND PURCHASE OF THE SCROLLS

THE dust had hardly settled over the battlefields of the world, when newspapers began to carry reports of a sensational new discovery in the field of biblical archaeology. It was announced that, in the summer of 1947, a cave had been found near the Dead Sea which had produced manuscripts of the book of Isaiah older by something like a thousand years than any previously known Hebrew copy of the Old Testament. Later examination was to show that of the scrolls found in this cave, the biblical manuscripts were probably the least important of what appeared to be the remains of a Jewish sectarian library dating from shortly after the time of Jesus Christ. More discoveries in this region followed in the ensuing years, and before long the world was in possession of the remains of hundreds of scrolls covering a period which had hitherto been one of the most sparsely documented, yet important, periods in Man's history. Questions which had been hammering at the door of scholarship since the beginning of critical research into Christian origins could now be answered. This little book is an attempt to trace the general outline of results so far achieved and where further research may be expected to lead as this exciting new material becomes generally available. But first let us see how the discovery was made, and to do so we must travel to the wilderness of Judaea, to a point amongst the mountains bordering the Dead Sea, a few miles south of Jericho.

Muhammad Adh-Dhib had lost a goat. The lad was a member of the Ta'amireh tribe of semi-Bedouin who range the wilderness between Bethlehem and the Dead Sea (see map on p. 10), and he had been out all this summer's day tending the animals entrusted to his care. Now one of them had wandered, skipping into the craggy rocks above. Muhammad pulled himself wearily up the limestone cliffs, calling the animal as it went higher and higher in search of food. The sun became hotter, and finally the lad threw himself into the shade of an overhanging crag to rest awhile. His eye wandered listlessly over the glaring rocks and was suddenly arrested by a rather queerly placed hole in the cliff face, hardly larger than a man's head (pl. 2). It appeared to lead inwards to a cave, and yet was too high for an ordinary cave entrance, of which there were hundreds round about. Muhammad picked up a stone and threw it through the hole, listening for the sound as it struck home. What he heard brought him sharply to his feet. Instead of the expected thud against solid rock, his sharp ears had detected the metallic ring of pottery. He listened a moment, and then tried again, and again there could be no doubt that his stone had crashed among potsherds. A little fearfully the Bedouin youth pulled himself up to the hole, and peered in. His eyes were hardly becoming used to the gloom when he had to let himself drop to the ground. But what he had seen in those few moments made him catch his breath in amazement. On the floor of the cave, which curved back in a natural fault in the rock, there were several large, cylindrical objects standing in rows. The boy pulled himself up again to the hole, and holding on until his arms and fingers were numb, saw, more clearly this time, that they were large, wide-necked jars, with broken pieces strewn all about them (pl. 1). He waited no longer, but dropped to the ground and was off like a hare, his goat and flock forgotten in a frantic desire to put as much distance between himself and this jinn-ridden cave as possible. For who else but a desert spirit could be living in such a place with an entrance too small for a man?

That night Muhammad discussed his discovery with a friend who, being the elder, was entitled to scoff at the superstitions of his junior. He urged Muhammad to take him to the spot, and the next day the two of them went to the cave, and this time squeezed through the hole and dropped inside. It was just as the younger lad had described. The jars stood in rows on each side of the narrow cave, and, in the middle, broken sherds lay amidst debris fallen from the roof. There were seven or eight of the jars all told, and some had large, bowl-like lids. They lifted one and peered in, but found it empty. And so with another, and another, until in the third they saw a bundle of rags and under it two more. If they had hoped for the glitter of gold and precious stones they were sorely disappointed, for the bundles crumbled at a touch, and, pulling away some of the folds, they could see only some black tarry substance and, below that, folds of smooth brown leather. When, later, the boys had taken this booty back to their camp, they took off all the wrappings from the large bundle, and unrolled the scroll it contained, until, as they later recounted wonderingly, it stretched from one end of the tent to the other. It seems certain that this must have been the larger of the two manuscripts of Isaiah, the news of which was to set the biblical world astir. However, at the time it evoked little interest among its new owners who could neither read the strange writing inscribed on it, nor think of anything useful to which they could put the leather, fragile as it was. So for a time the Bedouin carried the scrolls about with them as they pastured their flocks and made what trade they could with their neighbours. These Bedouin have no real home. The world is their prey and usually their enemy. This tribe had been in the vicinity since the seventeenth century, and they have managed to eke out a sparse enough living with their few animals, now and again putting their detailed knowledge of the territory to better gain in smuggling. Until the area became effectively policed by the Arab Legion, they practised highway robbery when they could, and always found a ready market for their trading, legal or illegal, in Bethlehem. It was to this town that they made regular visits to sell their milk and cheese, and there, one market day, they took the three scrolls. Their general dealer happened to be an Assyrian Christian, by name Khalil Iskander Shahin, known locally as Kando (pl. 3), who, besides the small general store patronized by the Ta'amireh, owned a cobbler's shop next door. When the Bedouin showed him the scrolls, he evinced little interest, but thought they might serve as raw material for his cobbler's business. Later, after they had been kicking about the floor of the shop for some days, he picked one up and looked more closely at the surface. The writing was as meaningless to him as to the Bedouin, but it occurred to him that his spiritual guardians in Jerusalem might know more about it, and accordingly one day when he was going up to the city, he took the scrolls along with him, to the Syrian Convent of St Mark in the Old City. This much is certain, but it must be confessed that from here on the story begins to disintegrate, as love of truth on the parts of the chief actors in the drama gives way before fear and cupidity. One thing is certain, however; Kando began to realize that the scrolls had some monetary value and found out that the Bedouin had by no means cleared the cave. He and his accomplice George accordingly launched a minor archaeological expedition to the cave indicated by the Bedouin and collected at least a number of large fragments and probably at this time the remainder of the scrolls, making seven in all. After they had taken all they could find, they seem to have let the Syrian authorities of St Mark's into the secret. In any case the Metropolitan organized his own expedition to the cave, which proceeded to ransack the place, making a large opening near the ground, and pulling out everything they could lay their hands on. Of course, it will be realized that all such excavations were and are completely illegal under the laws of the country, whether of the Mandate or of the succeeding Jordan Government. All such archaeological material remains the property of the country in which it is found, until the Government directs otherwise. So complete secrecy shrouded all these operations, and much harm was done as a result. It is certain that the Syrians found some more fragments, but valuable archaeological data like linen wrappings and sherds from the broken jars they threw on to a rubbish dump outside. Kando had meanwhile deposited the scrolls in his possession with the Metropolitan, on a security, he now says, of £24; and these and some fragments the Church leader began to hawk round the various scholastic institutions of Jerusalem to get an idea of their worth. It seems that one of the scrolls was shown to the late Professor E. L. Sukenik of the Hebrew University, who kept it for some time and then set about finding the rest of the scrolls, which he had realized were very old and of considerable value. He made a perilous journey to Bethlehem, for by now the Jewish-Arab hostilities had become open warfare following on the withdrawal of the Mandate. There he seems to have contacted Kando and brought away three more scrolls. This gentleman now began to get scared since he was afraid that the news of the illegal excavations would leak out, and he would rightly be held responsible by the authorities. He therefore took the precaution of burying some of the largest fragments from the cave in his garden at Bethlehem! Unfortunately, the soil of Kando's back garden is somewhat different from the parched dust of the Qumran caves, and when later he went to retrieve them he found only several lumps of sticky glue.

Meanwhile, in Jerusalem, the Syrian Metropolitan was continuing his rounds trying to discover if the scrolls were really old. Finally, on 18 February 1948 he called up the American School of Oriental Research and spoke to Dr John C. Trever, who had been left in temporary charge of the establishment during the absence of the Director. He told Trever that during a clear-out of his library at the Convent, he had found some old Hebrew manuscripts on which he would like his advice. An appointment was made for the next day, and the Metropolitan sent round the scrolls packed in an old suitcase, by the hand of a Father Butros Sowmy and his brother. After some hasty comparing of pictures of other ancient Hebrew manuscripts, and complicated research into dictionaries and concordances, Trever discovered that he was looking at a scroll of Isaiah, and that as far as he was able to tell, it was genuinely very old. He asked permission to make photographs of the scroll, and after some negotiations did so. As he worked he became more and more excited, for if it was as old as a favourable comparison with a photograph of a pre-Christian Hebrew papyrus fragment would seem to indicate, then he was handling the oldest manuscript of the Bible ever known. It was only with great difficulty that Trever could restrain his impatience when, half way through the work of photography, he had to fulfil a long-standing engagement with the Curator of the Palestine Museum, then Mr Harry Iliffe, to go to Jericho and take photographs of a local excavation. However, he seems to have restrained both his impatience and his tongue, for neither then nor at any other time was any mention of the discovery made to the authorities responsible for the control of antiquities in Palestine, who alone could have taken adequate and immediate steps to safeguard the treasures and seal the cave until a properly organized expedition could learn its secrets. Rather did Trever urge the Metropolitan to take the documents out of the country, since the situation was fast deteriorating, and war was beginning to stalk the streets and hills of that unhappy land. It was not until November of 1948, when the April copies of the *Bulletin of the American Schools of Oriental Research* reached Jerusalem, that Mr G. Lankester Harding, newly responsible for the archaeological interests of Arab Palestine as well as Trans-Jordan, learnt that eighteen months before, a fabulous discovery had been made by the Dead Sea. By now photographs of the scrolls had been examined by competent palaeographers like Professor W. F. Albright and pronounced definitely pre-Christian, probably dating to the first or second centuries before our era. Excitement ran high all over the scholarly world, and in Jordan, Harding was now faced with an extremely difficult and urgent problem. The source of these scrolls had to be found, and if any related archaeological material remained, it had to be expertly examined at the first opportunity, not only to confirm the palaeographical dating but to determine the community from whose library they had come. Furthermore, it seemed not improbable that there might be more scrolls, and certainly fragments, since apparently some of the documents found were in a fragile condition with pieces missing from the outside and edges. But the original discovery had taken place so long ago that the chances of finding the source relatively free from tampering were very slight. The Metropolitan had succeeded in smuggling the scrolls in his possession out of the country, and had taken them to America. The Jordan Government, of course, demanded their immediate return, but by now the monetary values being accorded them in the popular Press were so astronomical as to persuade the Syrian Church leader that the chances of his returning were well worth sacrificing for the sake of the money he could expect to raise in their sale. The one bright light in the whole miserable affair at this stage was that he had agreed with Trever and the American Schools to allow them to photograph and publish the scrolls immediately whilst their sale was being negotiated. The Americans had told him, apparently, that if they were published quickly their value would be much enhanced. In fact, it declined, since once they were readily available in printed form the need for the originals became less urgent. The American scholars did, in fact, publish them, extraordinarily well and quickly, putting the scholarly world greatly in their debt.

Back in Jordan, Harding had gone immediately to the Palestine Archaeological Museum in Jerusalem, and in his capacity as Acting Curator instructed Joseph Saad, the new Secretary, to spare no effort in discovering the whereabouts of the fabulous cave and any other information he could about the find and the personalities involved. Saad's first call was to the American School, and there Dr O. R. Sellers, that year's Director, immediately offered all the help in his power. Together they went to St Mark's Monastery, despite the extremely dangerous nature of the journey through the Old City, where Jewish shells and sniping were making it near suicide to be out of doors during daylight. Slipping from shelter to shelter they finally arrived at the building which backs on to the dividing wall between Arab and Jewish Jerusalem, and there interviewed a person by the name of George Isaiah. It became clear from the beginning that he was not going to be very helpful, and, although he did not deny that the Monastery had organized an excavation of the cave, refused point-blank to disclose its whereabouts. Saad argued, cajoled, and bullied, but all to no effect, and he was just about to give up hope of gaining any useful information at all when, out of the corner of his eye, he saw one of the Syrian fathers approaching, a venerable saint called Father Yusif. When the old man had drawn quite near, Saad suddenly turned from George and asked Yusif what he knew about the cave. Before George could stop him, the old man began to describe the excavations and their whereabouts. George turned on him fiercely, but could not silence him before he had given at least a general idea of the cave's position. It seemed that it was somewhere south of the junction of the roads to Jericho and the Dead Sea, amongst the cliffs which border the Sea to the west. Now those limestone cliffs are honeycombed with caves and clefts in the rock, and the mountains rise nearly a thousand feet from the marly plateau, so that with a southern limit at Ras Feshkha about six miles to the south, a good deal more detailed pin-pointing was going to be necessary for the cave to be discovered (see map on p. 11). As Saad and his companion retraced their steps through the Old City, they discussed the next move. It seemed obvious that they would have to try the great stand-by of the East, bribery. Most things out there have their price, and it only remained to find out how high it was going to be. So on their return, negotiations with George Isaiah were opened, on the general principle that, if he would lead a party to the cave, he would receive a cash payment and the custody of any further scrolls found would be equally shared between them. These negotiations took a considerable time, involving many trips to the Monastery through gun-fire. Finally, when it seemed that arrangements were sufficiently far advanced, Saad arranged for the mayor of Jerusalem and his dignitaries to accompany them to St Mark's to witness the formal agreement. The party arrived on the day appointed and took their seats. Everybody asked after everybody else's health, and were asked in return, and Allah duly thanked. Coffee was passed round, and, after that, the customary small talk ensued, without which no Arab meeting is considered opened. Sellers was beginning to get restless, but Saad, raised in the traditions of the East, played the game in all its formality and was patient. At last, after the seventh round of thanking Allah for their individual good health, the main subject was broached, the terms stated, and nothing but the clasping of hands remained to seal the bargain. And George Isaiah would have nothing to do with it.

Sellers and Joseph parted gloomily at the gates of the American School, and Saad carried on to the Museum. Weeks of negotiation had produced practically nothing and, apart from its general locality, they knew little more about the cave than what had been learnt from the American *Bulletin*. Now it happened that the Museum at this time was in the hands of the Arab Legion, and Saad had to pass a ring of sentries to reach his quarters. He made a perfunctory greeting to the man on duty at the gate and then something prompted him to hesitate and look at the soldier more closely. He was a lean, dark-skinned Arab of the desert, of the type Glubb always chose for his picked troops, and Saad studied his face for a moment, noticing his long, straight Semitic nose, his short curly beard, and black smouldering eyes. He was a true son of the desert from the sandy wastes of the Hijaz, trained from his boyhood in desert lore and with eyes as keen as an eagle's. It occurred to Saad that if anybody could find that cave, given general directions as to its whereabouts, men like this soldier could. They would be able to perceive from an amazing distance any disturbance of the ground round the illicit excavations, and so detect the cave perhaps even from ground level. The idea crystallized into a plan of campaign, and waiting only to collect Sellers from the American School, Saad went in search of the officer in charge of the troops in the Jerusalem area, a Major-General Lash. He found this officer well prepared, for only a night or two before he had been discussing the problem with a Belgian United Nations observer, Captain Lippens, and had that day telephoned to Harding in Amman, asking if he would like him to send a few of his desert troops down to the area and search for the caves. Harding had agreed, and now with the added information Saad was able to provide, no further time was lost and a detachment of troops under the direction of an English officer, Brigadier Ashton, and a Jordanian Captain (now Major) Akkash el Zebn, was sent down to the road junction by the Dead Sea. Deploying from this point, in such a way that as far as possible no section of the cliffs at all visible from the littoral plain would miss their scrutiny, they set off slowly, working their way south. Within seventy-two hours, Akkash was on the phone reporting that they had found the cave, and asking for further instructions. Whilst waiting for Harding's arrival, Ashton plotted the cave and started collecting the pottery which lay round about, making accurate notes and drawings which were of the greatest help to the excavators later. Then Harding arrived, and together they made the first preliminary excavation. Harding confesses that when he first saw the cave he was dubious of its being the source of the scrolls, but the presence of undoubtedly ancient pottery made it worth investigating further. He asked Ashton to mount a guard on the cave until such time as a properly equipped archaeological party could be assembled. This was done, but the expedition was dogged by bad luck for days. Every time they gathered at the road junction it rained, which made the tracks completely impassable to their transport, and once it even snowed! Ashton could not leave his men standing about outside a cave by the Dead Sea for long, however, and it became urgent to mount the expedition, which finally started work on 15 February 1949, a fortnight after the rediscovery of the cave. Father De

Vaux of the French School of Archaeology, Joseph Saad, and two others joined the excavation, and the early finding of scores of small inscribed fragments of leather, together with pieces of the linen wrappings, and the sherds of dozens of the characteristic large scroll jars, in which it was said that the original scrolls had been found, soon made it plain that this was certainly a scroll cave, if not the original one. The damage caused by illegal excavations was all too plain; no hope could now be entertained of any stratification of the remains, and some of the most valuable of the pottery and wrappings had been tossed outside on to a dump. The number of jars originally placed in the cave was now seen to have been between forty and fifty, and if, as it was then thought, each of those jars had held several scrolls, then it became a matter of extreme urgency to find the rest which might still be in the country and perhaps suffering damage. In any case, there must clearly have been hundreds of fragments and these had also to be found and studied together, if they were to be of any use at all.

Another detective inquiry was instituted, and Saad given *carte blanche* to find and, if necessary, buy those pieces regardless of cost. It was clear now, as more and more reports came in from scholars studying the first scrolls, that every word of these documents was going to be worth its weight in gold, and, indeed, that was just about what they were going to cost before they were all finally in safe hands.

Saad went again to the Monastery of St Mark's, this time accompanied by Harding himself. The object of this inquiry was to find out the name of the dealer in Bethlehem who had continually cropped up in reports, but had never been named. If there were more scrolls and fragments about, he was the most likely person to know about them, and he would also know the names and tribe of the Bedouin who had found the cave. George Isaiah was a little more informative this time, but could not or would not describe the cave in sufficient detail to make its identification with the Legion's discovery certain, and refused to disclose the name of the dealer. Saad knew better this time than to waste much time over him. After the inevitable coffee, and inquiries after each other's health, with no more useful information forthcoming, they rose to leave, keeping their eyes open all the time for Father Yusif. It was as they were leaving the gate of the Monastery that they saw the frail figure approaching, and immediately engaged him in conversation on the cave. Unfortunately, they now seemed to know more than he, and still they lacked the name of the Bethlehem dealer. Then they had an amazing piece of luck. Harding had noticed that as they had been speaking to Father Yusif, a woman across the road had been showing keen interest in their conversation. Finally, she came across to them and spoke. Were they talking about the excavations of the Dead Sea cave which George Isaiah had organized about a year ago? Her husband had taken part in the 'dig', and had even been rewarded for his pains with a leather fragment, which the priests had told him was most valuable, although he had not yet discovered a way of converting it into hard cash. However, if they would like to wait a moment she would see if she could find him; he could not be far away. Saad and Harding looked at each other, and then to heaven. They finally ran the man, Jabra by name, to earth in a nearby coffee shop, and induced him to come along to the Museum. In the basement, the spoils of the official excavation of the cave were arranged on large trestle tables, and, bringing him near, Harding asked Jabra if he could see anything there that he recognized. The man looked long and earnestly over the table, and then a broad smile lit his face. Yes, this. Amidst the broken pottery and linen wrappings, the Roman lamp and the cooking pot, he had spied his own dear, long-lost but never forgotten cigarette roller. So another link in the chain was forged, the cave was now definitely identified, and it now remained to find out how much more Jabra knew. An Arab who realizes that he has partaken, however, unwittingly, in an illegal act, is a wary creature. Harding and Saad had somehow to win his confidence, if they were to obtain the information they so desperately wanted. Bribery was of course inevitable, and a generous tip went far towards loosening Jabra's tongue. He admitted that they had found some scroll fragments, and the Metropolitan had taken most of them away with him when he left. They tackled him about the name of the Bethlehem dealer; but at once he shut up like a clam, and for a long time would say nothing on the subject. Harding saw the fear of death in his eyes, and the man confessed that he was literally scared for his life. It took a great deal of alternate threatening and re-assuring before they finally forced the truth from him, and when they had let him scurry off home, Saad and Harding sat down and faced one another. Events now had taken a sinister turn. If Jabra's fears were justified, it meant that this dealer and his confederates were willing to go to any length to avoid interference in their territory. It was clear that from now on the game would be played to very high stakes, perhaps to higher values than mere money.

The journey to Bethlehem was an adventure in itself. To-day it takes only half an hour of smooth driving on a new tarmac road to go from Jerusalem to Bethlehem, and before the troubles a more direct road took only half that time. In 1949, with this in Jewish hands, as it still is, the make-shift route was long and dangerous, a dirt track which snaked far out into the Judaean hills by the monastery of Mar Saba. Transport was by donkey, and the journey took half a day. The morning following the interview with Jabra, Saad set out, taking with him two of the Museum guards, and reached Bethlehem shortly after midday. Leaving the guards and the animals on the outskirts of the town, he walked into the centre, feeling suddenly lonely and unprotected. From now on he would be working alone; any sign of official support, and every way would be blocked; the dealer, scrolls, and everything else would go underground and nothing ever recovered. But Bethlehem in those days, cut off from a central government by the fighting, was no place for an unprotected man to face a gang of desperate brigands, and Joseph hesitated a moment outside the shop which had been pointed out to him as Kando's. It opened, like all such eastern shops, straight on to the street, and behind the piles of vegetables and hanging kuffiyas, the bright sunlight did not penetrate. Joseph peered into the shadows but could see nothing from outside. Then he entered.

His eyes took a little time to accustom themselves to the gloom, so he did not at first see the men standing at the back of the room, watching him. One of them was rather portly, heavy-jowled, and dressed in the long Arab nightshirt type of garment, with a red tarbush on his head. His companion was an older man who stared at Joseph suspiciously from beneath heavy eyebrows, and glanced from time to time at his companion and the door standing ajar behind him. Saad realized from their manner that news of his arrival had preceded him and came straight to the point. He had heard that Kando knew something about the scrolls which had been found in a cave, and furthermore, had some of the illegally excavated fragments in his possession. There was a moment's heavy silence, and then the old man flew at him, calling him a government spy, traitor, and worse, pushing Saad against the wall as he hurled abuse at him. Joseph raised his arms to fend off his assailant, but, even as he did so, saw the other man slip out of the open door and shut it behind him. Almost immediately the old man calmed down, glancing behind him to ensure that Kando had got clear, but Saad knew now that there was nothing to be gained by waiting longer and left the shop to return to his friends. Now the fat was really in the fire. Kando knew what he was after and suspected him of being in league with the Government. The chances were that either he would try and silence Saad, or smuggle the incriminating evidence out of the country and make off, until things had quietened down. The safest thing for Saad to do would have been to make tracks for Jerusalem and his well-guarded Museum. Instead he sent his men away, and took lodgings in Bethlehem, determined to try and win his way into Kando's confidence. It was the act of a brave man.

Day after day Joseph returned to the little shop, engaging Kando in conversation at first on anything but the scrolls.

He made the acquaintance of George, who appeared to be Kando's right-hand man, and had certainly co-operated with him in the illicit digging. Slowly he won their confidence, and one day brought up the subject of the scrolls again. He hastened to reassure them that no ill would come to them from working with him; indeed, if they would trust him he would find them a market for their fragments which would pay well and be perfectly safe. After all, if they tried to smuggle them out of the country they might lose everything, including their freedom. They would lose nothing doing things Saad's way. The logic of Joseph's reasoning gradually had its effect, and the first suspicion gave way to a wary, but nevertheless, genuine friendship. When he finally left Bethlehem, it was with a promise from Kando that he would come and visit him at the Museum. On the journey back, Joseph reflected rather ruefully that he had not seen a single fragment during all those days in Bethlehem; yet, on balance, he was not displeased with progress.

Kando kept his word and soon after appeared at Jerusalem, and Saad in due course paid a return visit. This went on for some weeks without further mention being made of the fragments, and Joseph was almost beginning to wonder if Kando had already sold them or, indeed, had ever possessed any. Then one day, in the gardens of the Museum, Kando took Saad over to a shady corner, looked at him hard, and then thrust his hand into the grimy 'night-shirt' and brought out a wallet. Inside, as he slowly opened it, there lay a piece of inscribed parchment, about the size of three or four fingers. Saad took the piece in his hand and studied it. There could be no doubt that the writing was very similar to that on the fragments he had already seen and the leather on which it was written was genuinely old. He replaced it carefully in the folds of Kando's wallet, knowing that one false move now could forfeit in a moment all the confidence he had built up over these trying weeks. Nevertheless, as he watched the wallet go back into its home, he wondered if he would ever see that precious fragment again. However, the game had to be played out the hard way; if Kando had that piece he would probably have a lot more, and Harding had told him to get the lot. Saad showed his interest in buying the piece and any more that Kando might have, and on this they parted, Joseph reporting the new development to Harding. In a few days Kando returned, ready to take negotiations further. Who was Saad acting for? Joseph answered that an English Professor visiting the country was anxious to buy these fragments, but wanted more than this one piece; how much had he to offer? Kando, rather warily replied that he had 'quite a lot', and arranged a rendezvous at which Saad would bring the 'English Professor' and where Kando would have all the pieces in his possession. The place appointed was to be in Jericho, and, when the date and time had been arranged, Saad went off to find the mythical financier. It so happened that, working with Harding at this time as a non-technical assistant, was an Englishman, Mr Richmond Brown, who willingly agreed to take the part. At a preliminary meeting Harding handed over a thousand pounds in one dinar notes (1 Jordan dinar = the pound sterling), but told Saad to try and obtain all the fragments in Kando's possession for eight hundred pounds. The absolute maximum was fixed at a pound per square centimetre of fragment, but to try and ascribe any monetary value at all to this priceless material was extremely difficult. If this price seems outrageously high, it must be remembered that, at that time, the Syrian Metropolitan was asking something like a million dollars for the scrolls in his possession, and reports to this effect were being heard all over Jordan on the radio. The Bedouin and Kando were now well aware that these scrolls were considered beyond price by the outside world, and that their recovery was worth almost any amount of money. It should be also recognized that behind all these negotiations there lay the shadow of irresponsible people who were willing to buy illegally smuggled pieces for their collections or as souvenirs, or in order to make a profit on a further transaction. The danger of such loss was ever present forcing the pace, and thus raising the price. It was bad enough that the complete scrolls should be taken from the country, but at least they could be published as a unity, as the American scholars were doing so admirably. But with fragments, it was different. They could only be made of use to scholarship if they were kept together, and as far as possible reunited with their parent documents. A small piece of Dead Sea Scroll may look very nice framed and hung over the mantelpiece, but it may well ruin the value of other larger pieces, depending for their sense on the inscription on the 'souvenir'. Furthermore, irresponsibility is not the sole prerogative of tourists and dealers. At a later stage, one world-famous museum was willing to consider buying fragments smuggled from Jordan in order to have them in their cases, even though to have taken them would have delayed the publication of thousands of others, or, at least, reduced their value for want of the additional evidence. Happily the possibility was then foiled by the more responsible attitude of an Eastern University who procured the fragments and returned them immediately to Jordan. Thus at this stage there was little quibbling about price; the main thing was to rescue the fragments and give them to the world in as complete a form and as soon as possible.

Kando's choice in hotels ran pretty low. This was a dirty, fifth-rate hovel, and, as the two drew near, Saad could see that Kando was fearing a trap and taking no chances. Lounging on both sides of the street and round the entrance were some of the grimmest, toughest-looking characters one could wish not to meet anywhere, and they watched Saad and his companion through every move and gesture as they approached. Joseph felt the thick wad of notes bulging in his pocket, and thought they could not have been more conspicuous if he had carried them in his hand. The hairs on their necks bristled as they walked through the porch, trying to look unconcerned. Casually they asked a shifty-looking proprietor if Kando was there, and he motioned them to a room leading off the main entrance hall. Saad put his hands on the notes in his pocket, squared his shoulders, and the two of them walked in.

Kando was standing with George at the far side of the room. A table covered with a greasy cloth stood in the centre, and Saad noticed that, as usual, Kando had prepared for a quick exit with a window standing wide open behind him. It idly crossed Joseph's mind to wonder if they were as well prepared. A brief greeting did nothing to relieve the tension, and Saad asked abruptly if Kando had got the fragments. The man nodded and raised his eyebrows questioningly in return. In answer, with studied carelessness, Joseph brought out the bundle of notes, stripped off the band, and fanned them out on to the table. It was a magnificent gesture and Kando hesitated no longer but laid on to the table beside the notes a pile of decrepit-looking pieces of skin, torn and rotted at the edges, and covered with a fine white dust through which the ancient writing could just be seen. Saad passed them over to the 'English professor' who at once began measuring them with a pocket rule. The tension had now decreased considerably, and whilst Richmond Brown was at work, Saad engaged Kando in conversation. Brown's calculations actually brought the figure to 1,250 sq. cm., but following his instructions he said 'I can only give eight hundred pounds for this lot.' Saad looked at Kando expectantly, but the latter jerked his head and gave the click of the tongue which is the Arabic refusal. Then he began to collect the fragments together, and Saad after a while did the same with the notes. Each delayed the process as long as possible, hoping for the other to give way, but when they both had finished the silence remained unbroken. Saad walked to the door, followed by Brown, both wondering if Kando would let them go through that grim circle of henchmen with a thousand pounds in their pockets. However, they passed unmolested and started to walk towards the Winter Palace Hotel where Harding awaited them. Certainly they were alive, and had handled the precious fragments, but were they to lose them all for the sake of two hundred pounds? Harding, however, having heard their story supported their action, and was sure that the next day would see Kando at the Museum with his pieces, more than willing to sell them for eight hundred pounds.

The next day sure enough, Kando appeared. But he seemed curiously certain of his ground, and would not go below a thousand pounds. Saad said he would go and ask the 'professor' and stepped next door to where Harding sat in the Board Room, awaiting developments. Harding agreed to the price and Saad returned and gave Kando the money. Then part of the cause of his confidence became apparent, for as Kando handed him the fragments, he looked at Joseph and said, 'and give my greetings to Mr Harding.' Saad remembered then that, when the three of them had left the Winter Palace in Jericho that day, a bystander had stared curiously into the windows of the car. Of course, Kando now knew the secret of Saad's relationship with the Director of Antiquities, and probably realized that the 'English professor' had been a fake. He knew too that the Government meant to deal leniently with him so long as he played their game. Indeed, Harding still had much to learn about the finding of that cave, and wanted badly to know the names of the Bedouin lads who had climbed through the hole. It was by no means certain that with Kando's collection all the fragment material from the cave had been exhausted, and there was always the possibility that new caves in the vicinity might be found any day, now that the Bedouin were on the look-out.

Eventually, Kando told Saad the names of the Bedouin and their tribe, and in due course they were persuaded to leave their desert camps and come to Amman. There Harding learned the full story of the discovery, and the Bedouin found a new friend in the Director of Antiquities. Well dined and liberally tipped, the lads returned to their shepherding to enliven the camp fires of their tribe with marvellous tales of the great city across the Jordan, and of an English official of their Government who spoke their tongue as well as they, and knew their customs and their lore better than any foreigner they had ever met. The wise administrator knows when to put the letter of the law into second place, and to the fact that Harding is such a person, the world owes much of the light which further discoveries in the Judaean desert were to throw upon this important Jewish sect by the Dead Sea.

CHAPTER TWO

FURTHER DISCOVERIES

Two years later, in the autumn of 1951, some Bedouin of the Ta'amireh tribe appeared at the Jerusalem Museum bringing a piece of leather sandal and a scroll fragment the size of the palm of a hand. They told Joseph Saad that these objects had been found in another cave some distance from the first, and it was eventually confirmed that they had come from the Wady Darajeh or Murabba'at (see map on p. 10). Four caves, high up in the near vertical face of the Wady (pl. 4, 5), produced altogether some of the most amazing archaeological treasure ever discovered in Palestine, ranging from a chalcolithic adze handle of wood (pl. 6) to two letters written by the leader of the second Jewish Revolt, Simon ben Kochebah (pl. 7). All the material from Murabba'at which had been taken by the Bedouin has now been bought back, and tells a story which, although quite unconnected with the 1947 finds of the shepherd boy, is exciting enough (see Appendix III).

It was nearly three months after the visit of the Bedouin to the Museum before official excavations could be started, taking place in January and February, 1952. Some of the clandestine diggers were employed by the official party, but whilst they were earning their honest bread, their brethren were continuing the great Scroll Hunt with added zeal. Eleven miles to the north, they were busy again in the vicinity of the 1947 cave, and even while Harding and De Vaux worked at the Murabba'at caves, news came through of another find in the Qumran region. Harding immediately went to the area on his own, and not far from the site of the first cave, saw the tell-tale cloud of dust from high up in the cliffs (pl. 8) which betokened the activities of the Ta'amireh archaeologists. There was nothing he could do on his own, so, turning his car, he made as good a speed as possible to Jericho and begged the services of two soldiers of the Arab Legion. With these he was able to round up four of the diggers, but the rest melted away, taking with them any fragments they may have had. These were later bought through the usual channels, but in the meantime it was decided to take the initiative from the Bedouin and organize an expedition to cover the whole of the Qumran area, searching for more caves and fully excavating the one recently found. The French and American Schools combined their resources for this work and covered an area for some five miles along the cliffs, exploring over two hundred caves or clefts in the rock. The clearing of the Second Cave produced very little more inscribed material and, apart from the famous 'copper scroll' from the Third Cave (pl. 10–12) which was found together with some leather fragments, no more written documents were discovered by this expedition, which is described in more detail in the next chapter. With the purchase of the Murabba'at cache and the fragments from the Second Cave, the resources of the Museum and the French School were pretty well exhausted; indeed, Harding had borrowed several thousand pounds from the bank on behalf of the Museum in order to buy what he had, trusting that when the full realization of what was happening became known to the world, money would soon flow in to replace it.

It was thus with some apprehension, as well as excitement, that some months later on 18 September 1952, Harding received a telephone call from Father De Vaux in Jerusalem saying that he had been offered an enormous quantity of fragments from a new source, and that after long negotiations he had purchased one lot for thirteen hundred pounds. The new cave was again in the Qumran area apparently, and Harding collected two soldiers and went straight down to the Dead Sea once more. Sure enough, there was the cloud of dust, and this time not in the cliffs but very close to the Settlement ruins themselves, only a stone's throw from where the excavators had been working that spring, clearing the remains of the buildings belonging to the Sect who had owned the library. That they had not spotted the cave themselves was not surprising, for there was nothing more than a small hole in the near vertical face of the wady to betray its presence, and the Bedouin had let themselves down on ropes to effect an entrance (pl. 14). As the car approached, the Bedouin made off with their booty, but on the way there Harding had waylaid the morning 'shift' going towards the cave (later numbered Four). It transpired that the tribe had been working in relays for about three days continuously, and had removed thousands of fragments, all of which had to be bought back, together with a small cache from another cave (Six), situated high up in the cliffs above the Settlement and the Wady Qumran itself. The archaeologists themselves found a small cache in Cave Four, overlooked by the Bedouin, and another cave nearby, numbered Five (pl. 15), but, all the same, a new and serious financial situation had arisen. The price was still standing at a pound per square centimetre, and although with all this new material it might be expected to drop somewhat, it was clear that tens of thousands of pounds were going to be required to save this fabulous library. Kando was now acting as agent for the Bedouin, who were themselves well aware what the fragments were worth, and demanded from him nearly as much as he could expect to receive. Gone were the days when he could make a thousand pounds for no more trouble than a brief expedition to a cave. The Ta'amireh jealously guarded their secrets now, and their cave hunting had become a thoroughgoing business, directed by the leaders of the tribe, and engaged in by all the able-bodied members. Nobody in the world knows that desolate area like these people, and it is certain that if it had not been for them the Dead Sea Scrolls would still have remained undiscovered. If the prices are high, the work is tedious and back-breaking in the extreme, and certainly no member of the expedition who scaled the cliffs and combed the hundreds of caves, sifting the dust between their finger-tips for days on end, in a stifling atmosphere which is just indescribable, would begrudge the Ta'amireh a penny of their gains. Furthermore, as more and more material became available, and the first close examinations were made, it became increasingly evident that these scrolls were fantastically important, beyond every scholar's wildest dreams. Already, study of the 1947 scrolls was producing any number of parallels with the New Testament, and these and the material from this and the later caves were clearly going to change every text-book on this period of Judaism and Christian origins that had ever been written. Even the tiniest fragment was of value, since the chances were that it could be joined to others, perhaps in a vital spot, throwing new light on the messianic expectations of the times, or the theological conceptions current among this Sect, of whom till now we had seemed to know practically nothing. Harding, then, rightly felt it his duty to save as much of the material as possible at all costs. From all sides letters came pouring in saying how valuable and exciting these finds were going to be. The newspapers carried long articles drawing the public attention to the miraculous finds by the Dead Sea. Harding himself could say publicly that this was the biggest archaeological discovery ever made in Palestine, and, taking into consideration this vital period in Man's history, there seem good grounds for saying the most important anywhere at any time. In short, the world of scholarship was brought to a fever pitch of interest and excitement, and articles poured into the learned presses all over the world. The only commodity which did not appear was money.

Harding appealed to his Government. Jordan's budget is ridiculously small when compared with that of Britain, France, or the United States. Every penny has to be put to urgent use, and development schemes cry out for attention if the meagre resources of the country are to be stretched to support an abnormally swollen population. With an enemy at her gates, she must for ever keep a standing army at the alert, which, even with outside help, drains her reserves intolerably. Yet, when confronted with the situation by their Director of Antiquities, who pointed out the value of these scrolls, particularly for Christian scholarship, this Muslim community found fifteen thousand pounds from its slender purse to buy scroll fragments. Let it be realized that this was not the careless gesture of some millionaire seeking social prestige among his countrymen. The money came out of the public funds and urgent agricultural and health schemes were delayed because of it.

But it was soon spent, and still fragments poured in from the Ta'amireh. Harding looked round desperately for more money. Clearly he could expect no more financial aid from the Government. People abroad were showing no practical interest in rescuing the fragments, though full of wonder and fulsome praise when they were saved. True the price had now gone down to half a pound per square centimetre, but thousands more were urgently needed. Harding had no option but to go again to his Government with what must have been an even harder request. If he could induce foreign bodies to buy these fragments, would the Government lift its very strict law against the export of antiquities and let the fragments leave the country once their message had been correlated with other pieces, joined wherever possible to their original documents and published? Obviously this work had to be done in one place, since once the pieces were distributed they could never be put together. But it would mean that these precious documents would leave their own country, and like too many of the treasures of the ancient East be sent all over the globe to be the pride and joy of foreign museums. It would have been natural enough for the Jordan Government to have refused this request. After all, there was always the hope that eventually some institution would give the money regardless of what they themselves would get out of it – considering the saving of this priceless material for mankind reward enough in itself. But the Government did not refuse. Harding was able to send a circular to all the great academic institutions of the world offering to 'sell' these fragments to them, providing the money was immediately forthcoming and that it was understood that delivery could not be expected until they had been completely edited and published as a whole. The first response came from the McGill University of Canada. A widow lady subscribed fifteen thousand dollars for the purchase of the fragments in memory of her husband. Then the Vatican in Rome gave about seven hundred pounds and, later, several thousand. A friend of Manchester University subscribed a thousand pounds, and the University itself doubled this amount. This money was gratefully received and spent, but still more was needed. In the spring of 1955, Professor K. G. Kuhn came to Jordan bringing with him fifty thousand German marks, about four thousand five hundred pounds, for the purchase of fragments. It was a fund raised jointly between the Federal Government at Bonn and the Government of Baden-Württemberg on behalf of the University of Heidelberg.

It took over three years from the discovery of the Fourth Cave to rescue all these fragments from Bedouin hands. In the spring of 1955, more scroll caves were discovered near the monastery ruins by the archaeologists, and numbered Seven, Eight, Nine, and Ten, although most of the material had unfortunately been washed long ago into the wady, and as late as the spring of 1956 the Bedouin produced yet another cave containing scroll fragments which had to be bought back.

CHAPTER THREE

THE EDITING OF THE SCROLLS AND FRAGMENTS

SEVEN scrolls were taken from the First Cave at Qumran: two manuscripts of the Book of Isaiah, a manual of creed and conduct of the Sect, a collection of thanksgiving psalms, an order of battle for an apocalyptic war between the Children of Light and the Children of Darkness, a commentary on the Book of Habakkuk, and another scroll which appears to be a pseudepigraphic elaboration of the book of Genesis, written in Aramaic. The Hebrew University had one of the Isaiah scrolls, the hymns, and the war scroll in its possession and released extracts from them in two successive editions of a small work. It was not until seven years had passed since they had come into Sukenik's hands that they published them in full with an introduction in Hebrew, and later with the introduction translated into English. In the meantime, the Americans had published the other Isaiah scroll, the Habakkuk commentary, and the *Manual of Discipline*, as the sectarian work was called, within three years of their arriving in the country in the hands of the Syrian Metropolitan. Unfortunately before they could get the Aramaic scroll opened, and it was in a very poor state of preservation, the time-limit set by the Metropolitan ran out and he refused to let them continue on the work. He seems to have been hoping that the one unpublished work among the collection would keep the price high, although it was not until 1955 that he managed to sell the complete set to a private purchaser, who bought it on behalf of the Israeli Government, despite the questionable ownership of the property, for something like a quarter of a million dollars.

The editing and publication of a complete scroll is a relatively simple task. The reading here and there may be difficult, but at least where the scroll is intact the position of the words and phrases is not in doubt. Very different is the preparation of hundreds of tiny fragments, many no bigger than a fingernail. All these must be laid out and minutely examined in the hope that they may connect with parent documents and be of use in reconstructing broken passages. The work of editing the fragments bought and excavated from the First Cave was entrusted to Fathers J. T. Milik and D. Barthélemy, both attached to the French School in Jerusalem. Starting work in 1952, the work appeared in 1955, having taken two full years to go through the Press. It is not surprising that the second-named collaborator was soon after flown home for extended medical treatment, although Milik has been able to continue on the work of preparing the Semitic texts of Murabba'at and, at the same time, by far the largest section of the fragments from the Fourth Cave. It is as well that the world should know the price in strained eyesight and mental fatigue which is being paid by scholars like these that it may have these priceless scroll fragments at the earliest possible moment.

As the Cave Four material flowed in, it became clear that its bulk was going to surpass by far anything found in the First Cave, and that it was beyond the capabilities of one or two scholars to edit in a reasonable time. De Vaux and Harding therefore decided that the work should be shared by a team of scholars brought to Jerusalem and resident there for this purpose over several years, or at least for one year with return visits of several months each. Since the excavations have always been carried out by joint teams drawn from the French and American Schools, with the co-directorship of Lankester Harding, an Englishman, it was further decided that the Scrolls team should be of an international character. Thus there have been drawn to Jerusalem for this exciting work men from America, Britain, France, Germany, and Poland, eight of us in all. The whole project has been a happy example of close international collaboration, and a wonderful experience for all of us (pl. 16). The division of work has been roughly that the two American scholars, Dr Frank Cross and Father Patrick Skehan, have taken the biblical section, in all the remains of about a hundred different manuscripts, Father Jean Starcky the Aramaic works, Dr Claus Hunzinger the copies of the War Scroll and some papyrus manuscripts, Father Milik the apocryphal and pseudepigraphal works, the Manual and Damascus Documents manuscripts, and other sectarian works, Mr John Strugnell the hymn scrolls and other non-biblical works, and myself the Bible commentaries and some wisdom literature. The material from the other caves has been put in the care of Father Maurice Baillet of France. Even when we are not able to be in Jerusalem, much can be done on the photographs which we take to our home countries with us, but reference to the original pieces is absolutely essential to the work, and, all the time, examination of the unidentified fragments is continuing and pieces are being extracted for absent members of the team and put aside pending their return.

Naturally to bring out and keep a team of scholars for such work from the four corners of the globe is an expensive procedure. Some of the institutions to which the members are attached have financed their travel and residence, whilst for others it has been made possible by a generous grant from Mr John D. Rockefeller, under whose patronage the Museum in Jerusalem was first built and continues its work. The results of our labours will be published in a series of volumes, of which the first has been that of Barthélemy and Milik dealing with the Cave One fragments and excavations. Next will probably be the volume of the Murabba'at caves, then fragments from the minor caves, to be followed by the biblical volume of Cave Four, and the non-biblical volume(s). Again the cost of publication has been defrayed to a large extent by Mr Rockefeller's grant.

The fragments reach the Museum from Kando or the Bedouin in cigarette cartons and the like, and are immediately stamped on the back with the code letters assigned to the various donors who have provided the money (pl. 18). Needless to say, that does not mean that those bodies will receive necessarily those pieces, for many will have been merged into their parent documents which may have been earmarked for elsewhere. In these cases as near an equivalent sized fragment as possible will be allocated at the final distribution to replace the other. The fragments then have to be cleaned of the white dust with which most are covered. Sometimes this is so firmly engrained that no amount of brushing will remove it, and then we find that a very light brushing with a camel hair brush touched with a non-acid oil, like castor oil, will make the marl translucent and bring up the writing very clearly. Very often it is not so much the dust that obliterates the writing as the colour of the leather itself, which has gone completely black from exposure to humidity and thus makes the writing indistinguishable from its surroundings. In these cases the process of infra-red photography has been particularly valuable in our work. We are very fortunate in having at the Museum a beautifully equipped photographic laboratory under the expert direction of Mr Nejid Anton Albina, who must by now be one of the world's foremost experts in this field. He used Kodak Infra-red plates and films, specially obtained from the United States, in conjunction with a red/violet, or a Red 3 filter fitted on to a Linhoff camera. Exposure at f.11 varies, of course, with the blackness of the subject and the distance from the lens, but to take our ordinary-sized glass plate of normally dark fragments (12 in. by 9½ in.) he sets his camera at about 32 in. from the subject, and gives exposures of six minutes between the hours of 8 and 10 a.m., and four between 10 a.m. and 2 p.m. A darker plate of fragments may need eight minutes, and exposures for particularly difficult pieces running over the hour are not uncommon. Such is the constancy of light in Jerusalem that he finds a light meter is unnecessary. Developing is done in ID 2 for five minutes and printed on soft or medium Bromide paper. The results on fragments where to the naked eye no writing at all was visible, are just amazing, and to this miracle we owe a very great deal of relief from serious eye-strain.

Very often the skin of the fragment is dry and brittle, sometimes tightly curled, and then it must undergo a process of hydration before it is safe to unroll it. The pieces requiring treatment are put into a glass vessel containing water at the bottom covered with a zinc perforated sheet and a sealed lid. After ten or fifteen minutes in hot weather the fragment is usually supple enough to allow gentle manipulation, but sometimes, with particularly coarse pieces, several hours of such treatment is necessary. If the piece is left too long, the result is a drop of liquid glue and one less epoch-making discovery. The clean fragments are laid out between the glass plates, several dozen or scores in each, and put out in the large room on trestle tables (pl. 20).

To the new collaborator entering the 'Scrollery' for the first time, the effect is rather shattering. He finds himself surrounded by about five hundred glass plates, packed with fragments of varying sizes, over which he will be spending the next year or two of his life crouching, trying to pick out pieces belonging to his documents, or seeking to identify new fragments. If he is a comparatively late-comer to the team, perhaps some of the results already obtained will strengthen his weakening resolve. In the corners of the room are the collected sections of other members of the team, and walking round he may see how pieces, no larger than the palm of a hand, have grown to cover complete columns of text, and whose secrets will be proudly shown to him by the collaborator responsible. He may look wonderingly at a biblical text which is going to bring about a revolution in our ideas of text transmission, or on a commentary which throws new light on the messianic expectations of the time. He may find himself gazing at the Aramaic text of pseudepigraphal work never before seen in its original tongue, and all around him will be biblical texts older by a thousand years and more than Hebrew manuscripts of the Bible previously known. He will have walked into a new and exciting world, but the way to the revealing of its treasures is a hard one, and before he can be sitting down reading columns of text and preparing the transcriptions and translations for publication, he has many months of extremely trying work ahead of him. Armed with one of his biggest fragments he will go slowly round those scores of unidentified plates seeking for the lost pieces. As he grows more proficient at the task he will be able to recognize a member of his flock from one letter or even part of a letter. One of the saving factors has been that of the four hundred or so manuscripts we have to deal with, surprisingly few have been written by the same scribe, so that by recognizing the idiosyncrasies of one's own scribes you can be fairly sure that the piece belongs to his document. Of course, this is not always so, and often we may find, after some months of patient collecting, that we have more than one work on a plate, coming from the hand of the same scribe. However, besides the script there is the rather less dependable criterion for identification of the skin itself. Where this remains constant over the whole scroll, it can be a most useful means of quickly recognizing parts from the same work. But, unfortunately, there are often extreme variations in colour and even texture where different skins have been sewn together to complete the work, or where disintegration of the scroll in antiquity has meant that different conditions have acted upon the pieces, so that one may be clean and supple, while its neighbour is darkened with moisture and warped completely out of shape. Warping is a major problem, for not only does it make pieces very difficult to join together even where the join is certain from the text, but it will distort the letters of the writing out of the true form, so that if there are only one or two letters on the piece, and the colour of the leather is changed from its parent document, it may be a long time before it is recognized as belonging to its own scroll.

Another cause of difficulty in joining is that worms or damp have often attacked the edges of fragments, so that real 'jig-saw puzzle' joins are no longer possible. This again is largely due to the scrolls having disintegrated in antiquity, and so frequently does this occur, and so often does one find tears which are certainly not new, that I am myself inclined to believe that the Fourth Cave was entered long ago and its contents maliciously damaged. Be that as it may, much of the relative positioning of the fragments in a document has to be done by 'dead reckoning' rather than edge-to-edge joins. This is not too difficult in the case of a biblical text where the order of the words is already known, although sources of trouble here are variant texts which we shall discuss in the next chapter. It is more difficult in the case of non-biblical works previously quite unknown or known only in translation.

An intriguing problem which has presented itself during the work has been the deciphering of a number of different secret codes in which several of the works were written. Happily they are nothing more complicated than new alphabets, which were composed by the Sectarians to keep certain works especially secret, and in one case they contrive to write most but not all of the words backwards, and use a mixture of four or five alphabets, including one or two of their own invention. Thus, for instance, one might come across a word written with a combination of alphabets in something after this fashion: X𐤄γיל Fע κעOβ ε𐤄X. The reader might like to work that one out for himself, with the clue that the alphabets represented in this imaginary example are Latin, Greek, Phoenician, and Aramaic, and the principle of using ancient letters for their modern equivalents is precisely that used by the author of this Qumran document. Having deciphered one column including a particularly puzzling phrase, it was encouraging to find another piece in a further purchase which contained the same phrase written, rather carelessly for the coder, in 'clear' Hebrew, confirming the decipherment.

Another code used entirely letters of their own invention, and begins in 'clear' Hebrew: 'the wisdom which he spoke to the Sons of the Dawn,' and then goes on into this unknown script, beginning 'Listen ye.' One day, when the three of us, who then constituted the team, were tired of cleaning the thousands of fragments in the boxes before us, we decided to enliven the proceedings by having a competition to see who could crack the code first. The main difficulty was that being very fragmentary there were very few complete words, so that determining the relative frequency of occurrence of letters, which would normally have given the answer in a very short time, would not work so easily in this instance. Some of the letters looked something like the protohebraic writing, a derivation from the ancient Phoenician script, but they made no sense when given these equivalents. Whilst Cross and I were tearing our hair over it after lunch that day, Milik strolled in and informed us that he had done it, or at least got enough of the letters to make a full decipherment eventually possible. He had guessed the meaning of one of the few complete words, which had the pattern *ABCBAD*. Since Hebrew is based on the triliteral root system there are not a large number of words possible with this combination, and a common group *LHTHLK*, the infinitive of the reflexive form of the verb *HLK* with the prefix *L*, meaning 'to walk about', gave him enough letters to break other smaller words, and thence to work through the whole fragment until he had the alphabet, or as much of it as could be obtained from the evidence available. There are, however, other cryptic scripts which have been impossible to decipher so far for want of sufficient material.

I have said that a factor which is apt to give trouble is the changing of skins part way through a scroll. Just as at times like this one wishes there had existed animals with skins large enough to suffice for a complete scroll, we often wish they had invented the fountain pen in the first century B.C. Some of our scribes seem to have had 'quill trouble', in that the instrument kept wearing down and giving the writing a quite different appearance from that presented when the scribe had newly sharpened his pen. I have one manuscript in my section, a commentary on Isaiah, whose writing changes startlingly in the first two columns, and fragments coming from later columns look different again. Of course, close examination shows the same basic characteristics are still there, but when one is looking through fragments of only one or two letters for pieces to match, these variations can be most puzzling. It is by no means unknown, also, for the Qumran Scriptorium to play a very mean trick on the Jerusalem Scrollery by changing horses in midstream, or rather scribes in mid-scroll. This is quite unforgivable, and most trying.

CHAPTER FOUR

THE BIBLICAL TEXTS

> There is, indeed, no probability that we shall ever find manuscripts of the Hebrew text going back to a period before the formation of the text which we know as Massoretic.

THUS wrote a very great textual scholar in 1939. Happily Sir Frederick Kenyon lived to see the wonderful disproving of his words in 1948, and would no doubt have been among the first to acclaim the later Qumran discoveries in the biblical field had he only been spared a little longer. For the fact is that with these finds from Qumran we have penetrated the Massoretic barrier by more than two hundred years, and produced texts from quite distinct traditions dating from as early as the third century B.C. To grasp some idea of what this means for the future of Old Testament text criticism, we should, perhaps, recount some of the basic facts about the transmission and versions of our Bible.

Our standard translations of the Old Testament are based on relatively late manuscripts going back no further than the ninth or tenth centuries of our era. As the very latest book of our Protestant Canon was written in the second century B.C., this considerable gap might seem to throw doubt on the reliability of our text were it not for the extraordinary care with which the Jewish scribes have transmitted their sacred writings. The most exacting rules were laid down in Talmudic works for the procedure to be followed in copying the Scriptures, and such was the accuracy with which this work was done in the synagogue rolls, that all the evidence available seems to point to a fairly consistent text tradition which goes back to the first century A.D. There was a very good reason for this. When in A.D. 70 the centre of Jewish life and culture was destroyed with the fall of Jerusalem, the religious observances of the Dispersion centred more and more on the Law, the first five books of the Bible, and its study took the place of the Temple as the centre of Judaism. It was therefore essential for the unity of the Faith that the text of this work should be standardized and given the authority of the one favoured recension, from which no serious variants would be allowed. A synod was convened at Jamnia, near Jaffa, between A.D. 90 and 100, at which certain disputed questions regarding the acceptability of some of the books were decided. At this time also, besides the extent of the Canon, the type of text to be used as standard must have been agreed upon, and perhaps even the type of script in which future copies of the Law would be written. Later, the ruling of the page, the size of columns, gaps between words and sentences and even the colour and nature of the ink to be used and the clothing worn by the scribe were determined for all time. Thus, from the end of the first century, the standard text of the Bible was more or less fixed and has been preserved for us to the present time with remarkably few variations. But it is important to realize that the Jamnia Synod did not compose a standard text, or even make an eclectic version from many traditions, but settled on one particular textual tradition as the norm for all time. They selected one from a number circulating in Jewish circles prior to that time, and it is in this matter of variant traditions of the pre-Jamnia period that the Qumran evidence is particularly valuable.

The new standard text, which, with all its deficiencies as well as excellences, has been brought down to us and which lies behind our English translations, is called *Massoretic*. Actually to apply this term to it in its earlier stages is an anachronism, for the very important work of the Massoretes, the body of Jewish scholars who systematized the *Massorah*, or 'tradition', did not begin until the seventh century. At that time these scholars set themselves to sort out the mass of traditional material which had grown up over questions of the true pronunciation and thus interpretation of the sacred text over the preceding centuries. In the Semitic languages in their early written forms, this question of traditional pronunciation is particularly important, for the text is furnished with practically no vowel signs, the nearest equivalent being the use of *w* and *y*, which approximate to the vowels *u* and *i*, and are thus used to denote those sounds. On the whole this defective system works quite well in literature with which the reader is well acquainted, and it is indeed surprising to the European student of the Semitic languages to discover how easily vowel signs can be dispensed with in reading. The real difficulties begin when the language ceases to be a living tongue and the consonantal text becomes sacred to the point where every word is regarded as of supreme importance for matters of faith and conduct. Of course, the forces of oral tradition as well as the natural sense of the context are usually sufficient to carry the reader along, but the size of the written body of tradition, which had been accumulated over certain difficult readings, was ample evidence that something more permanent and definitive was required to ensure uniformity of faith and practice among the Dispersion. Hence the work of the Massoretes, who, in imitation of the Syriac vowel system, invented sets of symbols for Hebrew and thus to a great degree 'fixed' the text of the Bible even more completely than Jamnia. But it must be appreciated that this 'fixing' was an essentially artificial process, since there still existed many different ways of reading certain words or phrases, and the selection of one in each case by the Massoretes, with an occasional recognition of another, was to some extent subjective, and the traditions they rejected often went back to a very early period, as we know from early translations and now from the Qumran documents. However, when we speak of the *Massoretic Text* (MT) it will be understood that we are referring to this first century tradition, embroidered with vowels and critical apparatus by the Massoretes of the seventh century, which forms the basis of our present editions of the Hebrew Bible and its translations.

The aim of modern biblical textual criticism is to establish, as far as possible, the original reading of the Scriptures, using all the means in our possession. These include, besides the standard Hebrew text with its Massorah, ancient translations which sometimes go back to the time before Christ, and certainly the most important of these is the Greek version. It is extant in manuscripts which go back to the very early Christian times and which contain works which, after a considerable period of uncertainty, were eventually excluded from our Hebrew Canon and now form part of our English Apocrypha. The history of this translation traditionally goes back to the third century B.C., when under Ptolemy Philadelphus of Egypt (285–246 B.C.), a number of Jewish scholars were brought to Alexandria to make a Greek recension of the Jewish Scriptures. The story runs that the king was urged to do this by his librarian, who had heard of the wonder of these books, and he accordingly sent an envoy laden with fabulous gifts to the High Priest in Jerusalem. His request made and granted, six scholars from each of the twelve tribes of Israel were selected, and the seventy-two worthies were dispatched to Alexandria to begin their work, carrying with them a copy of the Law written in letters of gold. After a wonderful reception, they set about their task, working separately at first, but later comparing results, and finally producing the Greek translation which henceforth became known as the Septuagint (LXX), or version of the 'Seventy'. The story later gained more fantastic accretions, and tells how the translators were shut up in cells, or by pairs in thirty-six cells, and produced a version in exactly seventy-two days, which, when subjected to mutual comparison, was found to be in exact agreement with one another, thus proving that the work was the inspiration of God. The general tradition does seem to have the kernel of truth that the work was done first in Alexandria about this time, and that the Law was the first to be translated. The other books of the

Old Testament were added later by different translators who varied enormously in competence and style, so that the general standard is uneven.

The LXX became at once the Bible of Greek-speaking Jews and had a wide distribution throughout the Mediterranean world. With the rise of Gentile Christianity, it became the Bible of the early Church, and since it began to be used by Christian theologians in theological disputes with the Jews, it soon lost favour with the latter, who began to prepare rival Greek versions. The most important of these was that of Aquila, made in the middle of the second century A.D., a most literal rendering which appears to be based on a Hebrew text more in accordance with that of the Massoretic text than that underlying LXX. This was keenly used by the Jews for debate and instruction, and its use was not scorned by scholarly Christians like Origen and Jerome. Half a century later appeared the version of Theodotion. His Hebrew text was nearer to Aquila's and ours than LXX's, but how far he relied upon the early translation is disputed, and it may be that recent finds in the Dead Sea area will serve to clarify the issue (see Appendix III). Theodotion's work had a great effect on the transmission of the LXX, particularly as regards the books of Daniel and Job, and perhaps others. On the other hand, it does look as if his peculiar Daniel text did not originate with him but was already to hand at his time, as would seem to be indicated by the new evidence referred to above. A fourth version was prepared by Symmachus, writing a short time after Theodotion. His main characteristic is a much freer and consequently a better Greek style, but the remains of his work are very fragmentary and his influence on the transmission of the LXX small.

In the first half of the third century, an Alexandrian named Origen, finding in existence three other Greek versions of the Old Testament besides the LXX, and often conflicting with one another, set about making a more perfect version than them all, and produced the famous *Hexapla*, or six-fold version, with the first column containing the Hebrew of the current standard text, the second the Hebrew transliterated into Greek letters, the third the Greek of Aquila, the fourth of Symmachus, the fifth of the LXX as revised by Origen himself, and the sixth the Greek of Theodotion. Origen's own revised LXX, the fifth column, later gained a currency on its own, very often less the critical apparatus appended to it by the compiler, so that in effect it became yet another version in its own right and considerably influenced the transmission of the text.

This much abridged account of the LXX's history will suffice to show that it has had a good many influences working on it to bring it to a closer uniformity with the Hebrew of the Massoretic Text, yet despite this, and this is the main point of our study, it is quite clear that at base it represents a different textual tradition from that of our standard Hebrew version which has reached us through the Synod of Jamnia and the Massoretes. One of the great questions of text critical scholarship has been, how far do the differences we find in the Greek version of LXX represent a different Hebrew original and how much the idiosyncrasies of the translators? Naturally, since we are dependent for our Hebrew text on a tradition which was standardized as early as the first century of our era, it is of more than passing interest to know what other text traditions looked like before this. Since, in many cases, in the historical books the LXX offers us a better reading than our Hebrew, we obviously want to know if the reading came from an original Hebrew text preferable at these points to our own, and if they do, then we ought clearly to give them as much authority as the one the Massoretes have bequeathed to us. There could be no question of accepting the Greek version of all the books of the Bible in preference to the MT, since a most cursory reading of other books, and in particular the poetic works, shows that they are on the whole little more than paraphrases, and not always good ones at that. The dream of scholars working in this field, then, has been to discover an ancient Hebrew text which clearly comes of the LXX family. Then, comparing this manuscript with the Greek of

LXX, they could see for themselves how the ancient translators went about their business, what they added of their own accord and what they left out, how sound was their knowledge of Hebrew and on what principles they dealt with difficulties in the text. But to realize this dream would mean recovering books of the Bible going back to the pre-Jamnia days, and indeed, as far back towards the time of the Greek translations as possible. Until 1952, this remained a rather hopeless dream.

Excitement had run high among scholars when it became known in 1948 that a cave near the Dead Sea had produced pre-Massoretic texts of the Bible. Was it possible that we were at last going to see traditions differing seriously from the standard text, which would throw some important light on this hazy period of variant traditions? In some quarters the question was raised with some apprehension, especially when news-hungry journalists began to talk about changing the whole Bible in view of the latest discoveries, but closer examination showed that, on the whole, the differences shown by the first Isaiah scroll were of little account, and could often be explained on the basis of scribal errors, or differing orthography, syntax, or grammatical form. For example in ii. 3, 'to the mountain of the Lord' is omitted; in vi. 3, the 'Holy' cry of the seraphim is given but once; in vii. 2, 'his heart' is missing, only 'the heart of his people' being 'moved'. Scribal errors of some consequence were those like the scribe's jumping from 'the vine of Sibmah' in xvi. 8 to the same phrase in verse 9, leaving out all the words in between. Sometimes he had added words, with another passage in mind, as for instance in xiv. 2 where 'and to their land' is made to precede 'to their place', thinking, no doubt, of the previous verse, or he adds 'and your fingers with iniquity' to 'your hands are full of blood', in i. 15, thinking of lix. 3. Similarly, in chapters xxxvi–xxxix there are brief additions recalling the differences shown in the parallel account in II Kings. The main orthographic differences centred in the much freer use of the 'vowel-consonants' mentioned above to facilitate reading, and this characteristic is general in much of the Qumran literature. The other Isaiah scroll showed an even closer following of the standard text, even to points of spelling, and there was a great deal of sighing with relief in some quarters, as well as sense of disappointment in others. Articles then began to be written about the support Qumran offered to the Massoretic text, and indeed these Isaiah manuscripts certainly did point once more to a pretty well unbroken tradition from the second century B.C. to the present day regarding this particular textual family. However, in 1953 came a discovery which was to put the matter in a very different light.

Whilst engaged one day in cleaning and assembling some fragile leather pieces of the book of Samuel from the Fourth Cave, Frank Cross noticed that at one place the text seemed to run completely contrary to MT. He checked again, and there was no doubt. He carried on brushing very gently until the next line came into view. Again the text showed marked variations, and the next few lines included a whole paragraph which was not represented in the standard Hebrew. His excitement mounting, Cross began to refer to the principal versions, and almost immediately saw that his text corresponded word for word with the Greek translation. The precious pieces joined to others, and time and time again he found positive correspondences with LXX against MT, until at the end of a week or so he was able to affirm that before him he had the answer to the text-critic's dream, a Hebrew text from the same family of tradition as that used by the ancient translators of the LXX. As the work continued, and more and more of the precious manuscript appeared, it was seen that sometimes it differed from both LXX and MT, and at others agreed with MT against LXX, but these cases were certainly in the minority. That scholars might have an idea of what had occurred, Cross published a portion of the new text in December of that year, and the following is an English translation of his reconstructed text side by side with the LXX and the Revised Version for purposes of comparison. The square brackets show the extent of his reconstruction, which, although it may seem at first glance to leave rather a lot to conjecture, is in fact less subjective than may appear. The very neat script of the scroll (pl. 21), a characteristic book-hand of Qumran, makes the calculation of letters and spaces missing comparatively simple, and when the beginning, end, or middle of the line is extant, reconstruction of the lacunae with a fair degree of accuracy, once the general character of the text is known, is of little difficulty.

QUMRAN	LXX	RV
I Samuel i. 22 – ii. 6		
[But Hannah went not up with him; for she sa]id unto her husband, *I will not go up* until [the child goes up when **I** have weaned him (?)	But Hannah went not up with him; for she said unto her husband, *I will not go up* until the child goes up when **I** have weaned him	But Hannah went not up; for she said unto her husband, *I will not go up* until the child be weaned, and then **I** will bring him.
that he may appear] before the Lord, and there abide before [the Lord for ever.	and he shall appear before the Lord, and there abide for ever.	that he may appear before the Lord, and there abide for ever.
and **I** shall gi]ve him for a Nazarite for ever, all the days of [his life.		
And Elkanah her husband said unto her], Do what seemeth thee good; tarry until [thou have weaned him; only the Lo]rd [establish] that which cometh out of thy mouth.	And Elkanah her husband said unto her, Do what seemeth thee good; tarry until thou have weaned him; only the Lord establish that which cometh out of thy mouth.	And Elkanah her husband said unto her, Do what seemeth thee good; tarry until thou have weaned him; only the Lord establish his word.
So the woman tarried [and gave her son suck, until she weaned hi]m.	So the woman tarried and gave her son suck, until she weaned him.	So the woman tarried and gave her son suck, until she weaned him. And when she had weaned him,
And she took him up to Shiloh when [. . . with a calf of] three years and bread,	And she went up with him to Selom with a calf of three years, and bread,	she took him up with her, with three bullocks,
[and an ephah of meal, and a bottle of wine,	and an ephah of meal, and a bottle of wine,	and one ephah of meal, and a bottle of wine,

QUMRAN	LXX	RV
and she entered into the house] of the Lord in Shiloh, and the child [with them,	and she entered into the house of the Lord in Selom, and the child with them	and brought him unto the house of the Lord in Shiloh; and the child was young.
And they came before the Lord;	And they came before the Lord;	
and his father slew] the offering	and his father slew the offering	And they slew the bullock,
as [he did year by year to the Lord;	which he did year by year to the Lord;	
and they (?) brought near the child;	and he brought near the child, and	
and he sle]w [the bullock;	slew the bullock;	
and Hannah, the mother of the child, came to Eli and said,	And Hannah, the mother of the child, came to Eli and said,	and brought the child to Eli. And she said,
O] my Lord, [as thy soul liveth,	O my lord, as thy soul liveth,	O my lord, as thy soul liveth, my lord,
I am the woman that stood by thee here,	I am the woman that stood in thy presence, by thee,	I am the woman that stood by thee here,
praying unto] the Lord.	praying unto the Lord.	praying unto the Lord.
[For this child I prayed;	For this child I prayed;	For this child I prayed;
and the Lord hath given me my petition	and the Lord hath given me my petition	And the Lord hath given me my petition
which I asked of him:	which I asked of him:	which I asked of him:
therefore I also have granted him	therefore I also grant him	therefore I also have granted him
to the Lo]rd: as long as	to the Lord: as long as	to the Lord: as long as
[he liveth he is granted to the Lord.	he liveth *he is* granted to the Lord.	he liveth he is granted to the Lord.
And she left] him there and she worshipped [the Lord		And he worshipped the Lord there
		And Hannah prayed,
and said,	and she said,	and said,

My heart exulteth in the Lord],	My heart is established in the Lord,	My heart exulteth in the Lord,
mine horn is exalted in the Lo[rd:	Mine horn is exalted in my God;	mine horn is exalted in the Lord:
my mouth is enlarged over mine enemies;	my mouth is enlarged over mine enemies;	my mouth is enlarged over mine enemies;
I rejoice in thy salvation	I rejoiced in thy salvation.	because I rejoice in thy salvation.
F]or there is none holy as the Lo[rd;	For there is none holy as the Lord;	There is none holy as the Lord;
and there is none righteous as our God;	and there is none righteous as our God;	
and there is none beside] thee:	there is none holy beside thee.	for there is none beside thee:
neither is there any rock like our God.		neither is there any rock like our God.
[Talk no more proudly;	Boast not, and utter not high things;	Talk no more, so exceedingly proudly;
let not arrogan]cy come out of your mouth:	let not high-sounding words come out of your mouth:	let not arrogancy come out of your mouth:
for [the Lord] is a God of knowledge,	for the Lord is a God of knowledge,	for the Lord is a God of knowledge,
[...	and God prepares his own designs.	and by him actions are weighed.
The bow of the mighty me]n is broken, and they that stumbled	The bow of the mighty *men* has waxed feeble, and the weak	The bows of the mighty men are broken, and they that stumbled
are gir[ded with strength	have girded themselves with strength.	are girded with strength.
They that were full have hired out themselves for bread:	They that were full of bread are brought low;	They that were full have hired out themselves for bread;
and the hungry ...	and the hungry have forsaken the land;	and they that were hungry have ceased;
the barr]en hath borne seven;	For the barren hath borne seven;	yea, the barren hath borne seven;
and she that hath many children languisheth.	and she that hath many children languisheth.	and she that hath many children languisheth.
The Lord killeth and maketh alive:	The Lord killeth and maketh alive:	The Lord killeth and maketh alive:
he bringeth down [to the grave, ...	he bringeth down to the grave,	he bringeth down to the grave,

QUMRAN	LXX	RV
Col. II. I Samuel ii. 16–25		
And the man would answer and s[a]y to the priest's servant, Let the priest burn the [fat] presently. and then take for thyself of all things which thy soul desireth: then he would say, Nay, but thou shalt give *it me* now; or I shall t[ake *it*] by force	And *if* the man that sacrificed said, First let the fat be burned, as it is fit, and then take for thyself of all things which thy soul desireth; then he would say, Nay, but thou shalt give *it me* now; and if not, I will take *it* by force.	And if the man said to him, They will surely burn the fat presently, and then take (for thyself) as much as thy soul desireth; then he would say, Nay, but thou shalt give *it me* now; and if not, I will take *it* by force.
When the flesh was seethed (?) one would take a fleshhook of three teeth [in his hand, and strike it] in the pot or cauldron: [al]l that the fleshhook brought up he would take. If [. . .] good except (in the case of ?) the 'brea[st that is waved' and the?] right [thi]gh.		
And the si[n of the young men] was very gre[at before the] Lord: for they abhorred the offering of the Lord. But Samuel mini[stered before the L]ord, being a child, girt with a linen ephod. [Moreover his mother] made [him a little robe, and brou]ght it to him	And the sin of the young men was very great before the Lord: for they set at nought the offering of the Lord. But Samuel ministered before the Lord, being a child, girt with a linen ephod. Moreover his mother made him a little robe, and brought it to him	And the sin of the young men was very great before the Lord: for men abhorred the offering of the Lord. But Samuel ministered before the Lord, being a child, girt with a linen ephod. Moreover his mother made him a little robe, and brought it to him

from year to year, when she ca[me up with her husband]	from year to year, when she came up with her husband	from year to year, when she came up with her husband
to offer the [yearly sacri]fice.	to offer the yearly sacrifice.	to offer the yearly sacrifice.
And Eli blessed El[kanah and his wife,]	And Eli blessed Elkanah and his wife	And Eli blessed Elkanah and his wife,
saying,	saying,	and said,
The L[ord] recompense thee	The Lord recompense thee	The Lord give thee
seed of this woman	seed of this woman	seed of this woman
fo[r the loan] which she len[t	for the loan which thou hast lent	for the loan which was lent
to the L]ord.	to the Lord.	to the Lord.
And the man went unto his own home.	And the man went unto his own home.	And they went unto their own home.
And the Lo[rd] visited Hannah	And the Lord visited Hannah	And the Lord visited Hannah,
and she bare yet t[hr]ee sons	And she bare yet three sons	And she conceived, and bare three sons
and two daughters.	and two daughters.	and two daughters.
And Sam[uel] grew before the L[ord].	And the child Samuel grew before the Lord.	And the child Samuel grew before the Lord.
Now Eli was very old;	Now Eli was very old;	Now Eli was very old;
ninety [. . .?] years of age,		
and he heard what his sons did	And he heard what his sons did	and he heard all that his sons did
unto the children of Israel.	unto the children of Israel.	unto all Israel, and how that they lay with the women that did service at the door of the tent of meeting.
[And he said unto them,	And he said unto them,	And he said unto them,
Why] do ye [such things]	Why do ye according to this thing	Why do ye such things?
of which I he[ar evil] things	which I hear	for I hear of your evil dealings
[from the mouth of all the people	from the mouth of all the people	from all this people.

QUMRAN	LXX	RV
of the Lord?	of the Lord?	
Nay, my sons; for it is no good re]port that I he[ar;	Nay, *my* sons; for it is no good report that I hear;	Nay, my sons; for it is no good report that I hear;
do not so, for the reports] which I hear are [not] good:	do not so, for the reports which I hear are not good:	
making [. . .	so that the people do not serve God.	ye make the Lord's people to transgress.
If one man should] at all sin	If one man should at all sin	If one man sin
[against another . . .]	against another then shall they pray for him	against another, God shall judge him:
to the Lord: but [if . . .	to the Lord: but if . . .	but if . . .

Two years later Dr Cross was able to publish fragments from another, older scroll of Samuel. Not only was this again shown to stand directly in the LXX tradition but it had the added interest of being probably the oldest manuscript yet to be found in the Qumran library, going back, as Cross believes, to the end of the third century B.C. (pl. 22). The LXX of the Law itself could not have been translated much before the date of this document! Briefly summarized, the results of the careful examination of these six fragments, which contain no more than about fifty complete words in all, are that, including three doubtful cases, Qumran agrees thirteen times with LXX against MT, and with MT against LXX four times. Impressive as these correspondences with LXX are for so small a selection of fragments, they do not, as Cross says, tell the whole story. The most extraordinary characteristic of this ancient witness to the text is the high proportion of original readings it preserves, which agree neither with LXX nor with MT.

Another interesting LXX-type text, this time from the Law itself, was also published by Cross's colleague on the biblical section, Father Patrick Skehan. It shows part of the Song of Moses in Deuteronomy 32, and from the appearance of the manuscript it appears that this song had once a separate circulation with arrangement of the text in hemistichs, a characteristic also of some canonical Psalm manuscripts from Qumran. Such a freedom in the treatment of the Law would have horrified a later copyist but appears to be nothing unusual among the Qumran scribes. Here again is a three-column arrangement of my translation of the latter part of Skehan's reconstructed text, together with the LXX and Revised Version.

QUMRAN	LXX	RV
Deuteronomy xxxii. 41-43		
I will render venge[ance to] mine adversaries,	and will render vengeance to mine adversaries,	I will render vengeance to mine adversaries,
[and] will recompense them [that hate] me.	and will recompense them that hate me.	and will recompense them that hate me.
[I will make] mine arrows [drunk] with blood,	I will make my weapons drunk with blood,	I will make mine arrows drunk with blood,
[and my sword shall devou]r flesh;	and my sword shall devour flesh;	and my sword shall devour flesh;
[with the blood of the slain and] the captives,	with the blood of the slain and the captives,	with the blood of the slain and the captives,
from [the head] of the l[eader]s of the enemy.	from the head of the leaders of the enemies.	from the head of the leaders of the enemy.
Rejoice, O ye heavens, with him	Rejoice, O ye heavens, with him	
and all ye gods worship him;	and let all the angels of God worship him;	
	Rejoice, O ye nations with his people,	Rejoice, O ye nations, with his people;
	and let all the sons of God accord him strength;	
for he will avenge the blood of his sons,	for he will avenge the blood of his sons,	for he will avenge the blood of his servants,
and will render vengeance to his adversaries,	and will render vengeance	and will render vengeance to his adversaries,
	and recompense justice to his advers-aries,	
and will reward them that hate him;	and will reward them that hate him;	
and will make expiation for the land of his people.	and the Lord will make expiation for the land of his people.	and will make expiation for his land, for his people.

Thus, in these small fragments, with no more than forty complete or near complete words of the Hebrew text remaining, we are able to confirm the existence of another divergent Hebrew text with strong affinities to the Hebrew recension underlying the LXX. From the above the reader will be able to notice some of the principles upon which the LXX translators worked, here a conflation, there a slight alteration to avoid giving offence, as in its rendering of 'all ye gods', as 'all ye angels of God'. MT avoids all reference to these heavenly creatures with 'all ye nations'.

Another version which has been used, with some caution, for textual criticism is that cherished by the small Samaritan community living at Nablus in Jordan, near ancient Shechem. It contains only the Pentateuch written in a formalized and rather artificially developed imitation of the ancient palaeo-hebrew script. The earliest manuscript hitherto known was that at present in the hands of the community and written probably in the eleventh century of our era, although the community itself believes that it dates from the time of Moses! Knowledge of this tradition in Western scholarship is comparatively late, the first copy coming to light in the seventeenth century. There followed a spirited debate on the value of the version as an independent authority for the text of the Pentateuch, until Gesenius in 1815 pronounced against the Samaritan version, maintaining that it was clearly secondary and offered hardly a single reading which was preferable to MT. It differs in about 6,000 places, but most are orthographic or syntactic differences, whilst others are supplements to correct apparent deficiencies in the text with the help of similar passages in other books, repetitions of speeches and the like from parallel passages, the removal of obscurities, and the insertion of explanatory glosses. It could often be shown that differences in matters of substance owed their origin to the dogmatic arguments of this Jewish sect, and could not therefore be regarded as original. But despite this, it was undeniable that here and there the Samaritan version did preserve some better readings, and it was not insignificant that of the 6,000 differences, 1,900 agree with LXX against MT. For example, in Exodus xii. 40, the 430 years of sojourning is said to have been in Canaan as well as Egypt, as in LXX (compare Galatians iii. 17). In Genesis iv. 8,

> And Cain said to Abel his brother, *Let us go into the field,*

is read by the Samaritan with LXX and other versions, and similarly in Genesis xv. 21, it gives

> and the Girgashite, *and the Hivite,* and the Jebusite,

with LXX; in Genesis xxi. 13,

> also the son of the bondwoman will I make a *great* nation,

as LXX and other versions; in Genesis xvii. 14,

> not circumcised in the flesh of his foreskin *on the seventh day,*

again in accordance with LXX and other versions.

These traces of genuine alternative traditions to MT made scholars hesitate before condemning the Samaritan version as late and comparatively worthless, and now Qumran has given it a remarkable vindication; for from the Fourth Cave have come fragments of the Pentateuch, written in a palaeo-hebrew script whose texts correspond in all essential points with the Samaritan version (pl. 23). Father Skehan has recently published a preliminary account of such a text of Exodus. In it, Exodus vii. 18 is followed by the beginning of the fulfilment by Moses of the command given him in vii. 16–18, which in the Samaritan version is repeated almost completely. Similarly, vii. 29 is followed by 'and he came' in the Qumran fragment, and is clearly the beginning of the Samaritan expansion which related the fulfilment of the command given in vii. 26–29. Exodus viii. 19 is again followed by an expansion which records the carrying out of viii. 16–19, and similarly again at ix. 5 and ix. 19 fulfilling the commands of ix. 1–5 and ix. 13–19 respectively. Exodus xi. 2 is followed, as again in the

Samaritan text, by an expansion which anticipates most of verses 4–7. In Exodus xvii. 13, Samaritan and Qumran add after 'his people', 'and he smote them'. Just as in Samaritan, expansions from Deuteronomy have been introduced into the Qumran scroll, and the Samaritan omissions of Exodus xxix. 21 and xxx. 1–10 are reproduced here also.

What this means, in effect, is that the Samaritan community have preserved a recension dating, presumably, from the time of the establishment of their own centre in the fifth century B.C., and which at least from the second century has remained virtually intact. However, as Skehan points out in his article, this does not change the overwhelming impression that it gives of being a secondary version. Thus its deficiencies, its free treatment of the text by additions and transpositions, must be recognized before it is used as evidence against MT. Nevertheless where it does show a better text its evidence must be given full weight, particularly where its support by the Greek shows it to have retained an earlier tradition than that of MT. In fact, once more, each case must be decided on its merits, and the Samaritan given the authority of a very early recension. A further incidental question which will have to be reconsidered is the use by a strict Jewish sect like that of Qumran of a recension which had been adopted two centuries or more before by the heretical Samaritans. Indeed, this is by no means the only link between Qumran and the Samaritan community, and is a question which offers a challenging field of research.

But it should not be imagined that the Qumran biblical texts follow necessarily any one of the versions consistently. Although this seems to be so in the case of this palaeo-hebrew Exodus manuscript, we have seen that Samuel varies somewhat in this respect and other manuscripts of Exodus and of other books of the Bible seem often to show a 'mixed' tradition. For example, another Exodus text gives marked LXX readings, as in i. 5 where MT reads:

> And all the souls that came out of the loins of Jacob were seventy souls: and Joseph was in Egypt already. And Joseph died . . .

and our new text, with LXX, has

> . . . seventy-five souls. And [Joseph] died . . .

(cp. Acts vii. 14, etc.). On the other hand other Exodus texts give readings which correspond now with LXX and now with Samaritan, and sometimes with neither. Similarly one well-represented Numbers manuscript shows an extraordinary text which goes with Samaritan, LXX and MT in turn, and is further characterized with a rubric written very neatly in red ink. A typical Samaritan reading is the insertion from Deuteronomy iii. 21 in Numbers xxvii. 23.

> [and he sai]d to him, Thine eyes have seen all that the Lord hath done to [these] two k[ings].

Yet in xxxv. 21 after 'he is a manslayer', Qumran has

> the slayer shall surely be put to death

exactly as in LXX, but against the Samaritan and MT. Then, again, two manuscripts of Joshua show marked LXX readings, whilst, coming into the prophetic texts, copies of Jeremiah show again a mixed text which will require further study to clarify. There are three relatively well preserved manuscripts of the book of Daniel, and the text seems to conform in most places with MT, preserving the transition from Aramaic to Hebrew in precisely the same place. However there are a few rare variants agreeing with the Alexandrian LXX against MT and Theodotion.

The overall picture, then, of the biblical texts possessed by this Community seems to be one of complete freedom of choice. They were not, like their later brethren, limited to any one text tradition, a state of affairs which, interestingly enough, obtains at Murabba'at sixty years later, where all the biblical texts found keep rigidly to the Massoretic tradition. Yet, even at Qumran, it can hardly be doubted that the MT type was gaining ground by its intrinsic merit, and it is certainly well represented among the biblical fragments from the Fourth Cave as well as the Isaiah Scrolls from the First. It was never inviolate, however. Changes from its prototype have certainly been introduced over the centuries of its transmission, whether from slips of the pen or deliberate alterations to smooth over inherited difficulties in the reading, or even to introduce readings more in conformity with the theological standpoint of the time. Sometimes in Qumran fragments we have a variant reading of a difficult passage which offers nothing in clarification over MT but at least shows that both texts found the same difficulty and tackled it in different ways. All this demonstrates that, although the standard text of our Bible is certainly very old and very reliable, it has not been without some scribal errors and 'adjustment' which will not allow for it any false claims of 'originality'.

How, then, is the new evidence from Qumran going to affect our Bible translations? It is, of course, early yet to come to any detailed conclusions, but certain fundamental principles seem inescapable. Whilst the versions have, from the very beginning of scientific textual criticism, been given their full weight by scholars in determining a more original text, it has always been the tradition in Protestant circles to base the popular translations on the Hebrew standard version, or Massoretic text, on the sound principle that it alone is the most fully preserved text in the original tongue. Whilst the Greek may offer here and there a better reading, its origins were always dubious, since we knew very little about the nature of the Hebrew text before the translators, or indeed if, in these cases, it really existed in a different form from MT, and the better reading were not merely the arbitrary emendment of the translator. Thus a Greek reading, even if clearly preferable for the sense of the passage, was usually consigned to the margin, on the primary principle that at all costs, even, all too often, of Hebrew grammar and lexicography, the standard text must be made to give sense. Only if all else failed and still no possible translation could be squeezed from the Hebrew were the renderings of the versions allowed to take their place in the text of the translation. It seems now that, to scholars engaged on this work in the future, Qumran has offered a new basis for a confidence in the LXX in at least the historical books, which should allow them to accept the better readings of that version almost as readily as if they were found in the Hebrew MT. In other words, each reading must in future be judged *on its merits*, not on any preconceived notion of the superiority of the Hebrew version, simply because it is Hebrew. If the Greek offers a better reading, then that ought to be taken and put in the text of the translation; if the Samaritan recension gives better sense, then that ought to be given first place, since we now know that it has at least as great a claim to antiquity as the Qumran exemplars of MT. This gives support to those scholars who would make an eclectic text the foundation of a future translation. The whole business becomes infinitely more complicated, and, it must be admitted, more subjective. And that is the difficulty. To make such an eclectic version demands the use of critical faculties on the traditions which many scholars would hesitate to employ on a popular version. They will say, with much justice, that to make a choice between two or more readings in a sacred text is a responsibility which no body of men ought to be asked to make, or even that it is possible to make with any hope of permanence. They will point, for instance, to the text criticism of only a few decades ago when the fashion in scholarship was then to regard as hopelessly out-of-date and reactionary the practice of leaving two verses standing together, or to do anything else with a corrupt text than to rip it out entirely and rewrite it as they themselves would have done had they been the author. Fashions in textual criticism change as in most other things, and little permanence could be expected from a Bible translation which depended so much on the personal preferences of a few scholars of a certain age. No sooner was one translation ready for the Press than a new set of translators would want to begin another.

This is all perfectly true, but the choice seems to be

between offering to the public as perfect a rendering as possible of an imperfect text merely because it happens to be the one complete Hebrew recension of the Bible we possess, and between using every faculty of modern scholarship to compose a version which, if it can make no claim to infallibility, at least has the merit of treating all the difficulties of the text seriously, glossing none over with impossible renderings in italics or otherwise, and making full use of ancient versions whose Hebrew originals we now know to have existed, and parts of which we actually have in our possession. The one way is safer for the scholar involved, since he can defend all his readings by reference to only one text, and he cuts down the area of subjective judgement to a minimum. To attempt the other is to invite continual accusations of partisanship and over-subjectivity in a matter which for very many people is a matter of personal faith. On the other hand, the cry for permanence in a Bible translation is a vain one these days. Hardly a day passes without some new light being thrown upon the meanings of the text of the Bible, new inscriptions are found or deciphered, archaeological excavations give us a better idea of how the people of those days lived, and all this affects our understanding of the text. We can never expect any translation now to be accorded the long-lived and undeserved authority of the King James version. Similarly the cry for objectivity is just as misplaced. Scholars are only human, and translations, from one language to another, despite the new electronic translation machines, are among the most subjective of man's activities. It is true that to widen the field of translation to more than one text is to risk more subjectivity in the answer, but the question is only one of degree. The public, one presumes, is more interested in having a translation which is as near as possible what the prophet spoke or wrote than an accurate rendering of a particular Hebrew manuscript. If Qumran helps us to satisfy that requirement, then I believe we should use all the information it can offer, even though it makes our work vastly more complicated.

In any case, the whole question must be seen in a proper sense of proportion. The comparative translations which have been given in the previous pages will make it clear to the reader that to use another translation is not going to change the whole face of our Bible. The differences are matters of detail and should result in a clearer, smoother text than the one we have been wont to use. And again, the principle of an eclectic text is not so strange. We have recently seen a very good example of what can be done in this way in the translation of the Scriptures offered by the Catholic Biblical Association of America. Here all the versions have been accorded full weight of authority and their readings, where clearly preferable, included in the text, whilst separate sections give full textual notes wherever the versions have been used in place of the Hebrew. The result is not only extremely readable, but a major work of scholarly erudition which might well be a model of future translations, whose collaborators will now have the support of the new Qumran material to give them confidence in their use of other recensions.

CHAPTER FIVE

THE EXCAVATIONS AT QUMRAN

The First Cave

THE surface of the Dead Sea lies at about 1,300 feet below that of the Mediterranean, some fifty miles to the west. Walking westwards from the shore, the visitor crosses the flat littoral plain up to the fallen rock which precedes the two abrupt rises of the cliffs themselves. These very steep slopes rise to within a few hundred feet of sea level, and the first cave is situated at the upper limit of the first of them. Although the site is fast becoming one of Jordan's main tourist attractions, the visitor may rest assured that it will be many years before he will be besieged by post-card selling guides and ice cream vendors. The area is completely barren, and although cars can reach the foot of the cliffs, from then on the visitor must climb the steep slopes on foot, and the sharp-edged limestone rocks are unkind to the hardiest shoes. The loose shale also makes the climb difficult, and parties should keep together at the worst parts to help each other where the going becomes treacherous. However, the climb is not impossible for the most sedentary tourist, but he will almost certainly need a guide to find the right spot to begin the climb. Failing this, he may be aided by the knowledge that, after crossing the first main wady north of Qumran, keeping to the track which runs beneath the cliffs, he will come upon the circles of stones marking the site of the camp of the 1949 excavators. A little farther on he will note on his right a large boulder standing on its own in the plain, and looking towards the left he will see another at the foot of the cliffs. Taking a bearing through these stones, he will be led to the heap of tumbled shale which is the beginning of the climb. If he keeps going straight up from here he cannot miss the cave on his right, behind a pinnacle of rock.

Entrance can now be made easily through the narrow vertical opening enlarged by the clandestine excavators, and above can be seen the hole through which the Bedouin lad threw the stone. Inside, of course, the floor has been completely turned over, but otherwise the cave differs little from how it must have looked in 1947 when Muhammad lost his goat (pl. 2).

Official excavations, under the leadership of Mr Lankester Harding, and Father De Vaux of the French School of Archaeology in Jerusalem, began on 15 February 1949 and continued until 5 March. First to be examined was the dump left by the clandestine diggers, and this yielded large quantities of sherds and linen scroll wrappings, and a few pieces of inscribed leather, including the first fragment recovered from Qumran written in the old proto-hebraic or 'Phoenician' characters, and representing part of the text of Leviticus. The filling of the cave itself consisted of a fine powdery dust, and stones fallen from the sides and roof of the cave. Every ounce of this material had to be minutely examined with nothing more mechanical than a pair of tweezers and a camel hair brush, for the slightest pressure will often break the scroll fragments even further, and being covered with this marly deposit, they are easily missed amongst the debris.

The documentary results of this exacting toil produced hundreds of pieces, ranging in size from those smaller than a fingernail to fragments containing several lines of writing. As they were found, the pieces were carefully placed between glass plates and taken to the Jerusalem Museum for photographing. A part of a scroll, now completely coagulated with damp into a mass of glue, was found adhering to the collar of a broken jar, and still covered with its linen wrapper. Small leather phylactery cases were found, made in two parts stitched together, forming four small pouches into which minute rolls of very fine parchment had once been placed. These, inscribed with certain portions of the Old Testament, were believed to act as a sort of charm for the wearer. Single compartment phylacteries were also found, and, among the fragments, the remains of a phylactery itself, though from its size unlikely to have belonged to any of the cases found. Two fragments of a wooden comb were also found, which seem to indicate that perhaps this cave was anciently used for a dwelling place as well as a deposit for the library.

By this time all the intact jars had been taken away or broken. Professor Sukenik had purchased two from Kando, and I myself bought another from him in 1953 which was quite intact, apart from a small hole near the bottom sealed with pitch, and which had probably been used all this time by the Bedouin in their camp as a storage vessel. Some of the sherds recovered showed signs of recent breakage, probably received during the clandestine pillage, but patient work in the Museum restored many jars to their original shape, and some were later sold to Museums all over the world (pl. 1). Other pieces of pottery included the parts of several bowl-like jar lids, some bowls, a cooking pot, a small jug, and several lamps.

The scroll jars themselves came to assume a magnified importance for the archaeologists, who were particularly concerned at this stage in finding some criteria by which the cave deposit might be dated. The difficulty was that the jars were practically unique in shape and size. Generally between 21 in. and 27 in. long, they were cylindrical in shape, flattening sharply at top and bottom to a wide collared neck and ring base respectively. Marks of turning are clearly visible on the sides, and the deep firing has given the pottery a hard, almost metallic quality, with a characteristic rose pink or grey colouring. Some of the jars vary somewhat from this general pattern, being smaller and with rather more bulging sides, whilst one has a rounded bottom. Another characteristic of the smaller jars are the handles on the shoulders, sometimes small and vertical like those of a cup, but other times nothing more than horizontal lugs, pierced with holes through which string could be passed to retain the lid in position. When at a later date such smaller jars were found in the ruins of the Settlement itself, it was realized that they must have been storage jars, and thus not necessarily used for preserving written documents, so that it could no longer be maintained that all the forty or fifty vessels found represented in the first cave were essentially 'scroll jars'.

The nearest parallel to the characteristic large jars of Qumran is certainly to be seen in vessels found in Egypt at the beginning of this century and similarly containing documentary material which could be dated to the second century B.C. It is not improbable, therefore, that the general shape of the jars and idea of scroll storage were borrowed by the Qumran sect from Egypt, and this is by no means the only indication of a fairly close contact between it and that area. But certainly for Palestinian ceramics, these jars were unique. However, the other pottery found in the cave could be matched with discoveries made elsewhere in the country. The cooking pot and the narrow-necked juglet were closely similar to those found in Jewish tombs in the environs of Jerusalem and elsewhere, dating to late Hellenistic or Roman times, i.e., from the first half of the first century B.C. down to the fall of Jerusalem in A.D. 70. Two of the lamps seemed to be Hellenistic in general appearance, but another couple were certainly no earlier than Roman. At first this was interpreted by the archaeologists as pointing to a Hellenistic date for the deposit with a later Roman entry. However, after excavations had been made on the ruined Settlement itself, where more jars were found and where coins gave an exact final dating for the main period of occupation to A.D. 68, it was conceded that the early dating of the cave was probably wrong, and the deposit there would have to be brought down also to Roman times. The earlier types of the lamps must then be attributed to later copying. Now that we have been able to examine the palaeographical evidence afforded by the remains of hundreds more scrolls from other caves in the area, everything seems to substantiate this dating, and certainly none of the literary evidence so far obtained from the fragments militates against it.

The practice of putting scrolls in jars for safe storage was by no means uncommon in antiquity, and in his report on the archaeology of the first cave, Father De Vaux recalls instances ranging from the time of Rameses III down to an Arab letter of the eighth or ninth century of our era where the practice is referred to. Unfortunately our Qumran community did not always use this admirable method, and in other caves the scrolls had been left without such protection so that they have deteriorated to fragments by the ravaging of animals and the elements. Why the Sectarians should have put some into jars and left others without adequate protection is a puzzle. The answer probably is that some had been put away properly with a view to their preservation and perhaps future use, whilst others had been thrown into the nearest hiding place available at the approach of the enemy who finally forced them to flee. But it seems not improbable that some of the caves where fragments were found had been dwelling places of members of the Sect, who had left their own private copies of the Scriptures in them, and abandoned them at the last moment, perhaps because they had no time to return to their caves.

The puzzle of the uniqueness of the jars in Palestine was solved when the archaeologists found in the ruins of the Settlement a pottery kiln (pl. 31), showing that in this, as in many other things, the Sect tried to be as independent of the outside world as possible. Working to Egyptian patterns they had probably adapted them to their own use and thus produced a type of pottery which could not be paralleled elsewhere in Palestine.

The flaxen scroll coverings recovered from the cave were sent to Mrs G. M. Crowfoot for expert examination, and her report in the Cave One volume of the *Discoveries in the Judaean Desert* makes interesting reading. All the fragments appear to have come from small cloths, definitely shaped and sewn. Some were certainly designed as scroll wrappers, while others had been folded into pads and may have formed a packing for the scrolls inside the jars. Other pieces were found with twisted corners tied with string, and doubtless served as jar covers tied across the open necks. Some of the cloths were decorated with blue lines, and the Shirley Institute of Manchester found, on examination, that the dye used was certainly indigo. The usual form of decoration consists of simple blue lines in the weft, generally of two wefts only, although, in the case of one piece, the weft is double, and, on another, an embroidered line is added. There was only one piece found with a more elaborate pattern complete, a design of rectangles within one another, but there is evidence that this design was attempted on other less well-preserved cloths. Jewish writings give ample evidence for the working of flax between the second century B.C. and the second A.D. in Palestine, and Mrs Crowfoot's conclusion is that the linen of the scroll cave is a local product. Although in some respects, rather like the scroll jars, it shows similarities with the Egyptian variety, there are essential differences which give it a rather more coarse appearance. By a very careful examination of the materials, Mrs Crowfoot also hazards the opinion that the loom used was a rather primitive warp weighted upright structure, although the type with an upper and lower beam was probably in use at this time in Palestine as elsewhere.

Another interesting examination of the flaxen textiles was carried out, this time in the laboratories of the University of Chicago, by Dr W. F. Libby. The object of these experiments was the determination by radiological means of the date at which the flax was cut. This almost incredible possibility was made feasible by the discovery that an atomically unstable form of Carbon, whose atomic weight is 14 instead of the normal 12, was continually being created in the earth's upper atmosphere by the bombardment of cosmic rays on Nitrogen-14 atoms. The resultant Carbon-14 combines with oxygen to make a particular form of carbon dioxide, which becomes mixed with normal carbon dioxide in definite proportions. Thus Carbon-14 is breathed by all living plants and animals in their various life processes, and as a result, as Libby showed in 1946, all such creatures contain a constant proportion of the unstable Carbon-14, in the proportion of about one trillionth of a gram of Carbon-14 to one gram of Carbon-12. With death, of course, the intake of Carbon-14 comes to an end, but the amount in the body remains and slowly disintegrates at a constant rate. The 'half-life' of Carbon-14 is 5,500 years, so that one ounce would become half an ounce in that length of time, a quarter of an ounce in the next 5,500 years, and so on. It will be clear that if the amount remaining in a specimen of organic matter can be accurately measured, the time since it ceased to breathe in this heavy form of Carbon can be estimated without difficulty. The laboratory procedure is to burn the sample to pure carbon, and then measure the residue with an extremely sensitive radiation meter on the Geiger counter principle. The measurement is expressed in terms of the number of Carbon-14 disintegrations per minute per gram of carbon. This value is 15.3 for a contemporary living sample, 7.65 for a sample 5,508 years old, 3.83 for a sample 11,136 years old and so on. But it is not surprising to know that in calculating such infinitesimal quantities a margin of error must be allowed for which increases with the age of the sample. The acknowledged error is between 5 and 10 per cent, and the limit of measurable range 20,000 years. It seems likely, however, that new methods will cut the margin of error considerably and increase the range. Although Carbon-14 is present in all organic matter, it appears that certain kinds of material have been found most amenable to the test, such as plant growth, like wood and charcoal, shell, antler and burned bone, dung and peat. Tests made on material which can be otherwise dated have brought some amazingly accurate results. A slab of wood from the roof beam of an Egyptian vizier's house of the First Dynasty, variously dated between 3100 and 2800 B.C. averaged, over two 'runs', 2933 with a margin of error of 200 years, and a piece of deck planking from the funeral boat of King Sesostris III, who died about 1849 B.C., gave a reading which brought this date well within the marginal errors. It was thus with some excitement that the results from the flaxen scroll covers of the first cave were awaited. Dr Libby announced that from his calculations the flax used in the material was cut in A.D. 33, with a margin of error of plus or minus 200 years, i.e. within the range A.D. 233 and 168 B.C. (there being of course, no year '0'). So near is this central date for what, on other evidence, must be the time of the preparation of the cloths, that the result is almost breathtaking, and opens up a wonderful prospect of accuracy in archaeological dating of the future.

The ink used on the scrolls was tested in the British Museum research laboratories by Dr H. J. Plenderleith, who found it to be of a carbon composition, resistant to mild bleaching, and one may add, to a surprising amount of hard brushing which attempts at reading and matching have made necessary at times. There has been very little fading of the writing on the fragments, and in many cases it stands out as freshly as the day it was written.

The leather of the fragments was tested in the Department of Leather Industries of the University of Leeds, to whose Director, Dr Donald Burton, a box of blank samples was sent for expert examination. The nature of the skins and the grouping of the hair follicles indicated young goats and lambs as the main source of the material, which would not rule out the possibility that the Qumran community was preparing their own writing materials. Although the immediate surroundings of the caves are barren enough, the spring of 'Ain Feshkha, not more than a mile to the south, had always been an abundant source of fresh water herbage, and Jericho to the north could have provided all the tannin substances necessary for the work.

The Monastery

During the excavations of the cave in the early spring of 1949, De Vaux and Harding had naturally looked around for some evidence of human habitation nearby which might be connected with the deposit of scrolls. About a thousand yards to the SSE. of the first cave they discovered the ruins of a building standing on a plateau midway between the sea and the cliffs (pl. 9 and map on p. 11). This *Khirbet*, as such ruins are called locally, had been seen before by travellers and mentioned in their reports. De Saulcy, in 1851, had suggested they might be the remains of the biblical Gomorrah, which must surely have made our pious Sectarians turn in their graves. The first valuable description was given by Clermont Ganneau in 1873, and Dalman correctly recognized Roman remains on the spot in his report of 1920. Martin Noth has recently suggested with much plausibility that the site and general area represents the ancient 'City of Salt' mentioned in Joshua xv. 62. But the ruins remained virtually untouched until Harding and De Vaux decided to make a trial sounding in 1949, and dug out two of the tombs in the adjacent cemetery. This extends to the east of the ruins and contains about a thousand graves, nearly all of which were orientated north and south. This fact is very strange in a Muslim country, and Clermont Ganneau had commented on the peculiarity, suggesting that they must date from pre-Islamic times. They are marked by a simple oval of stones, with an occasional dressed stone at the extremities, and when excavated proved to be of extremely simple construction, with practically no grave furniture at all. A shaft had been dug through the pebbles of the marine terrace and through the marl below to a depth which varied between four and six feet. At the bottom, the grave itself had been dug usually into the eastern side and then covered with crude bricks of unburnt clay or simply stones. The body had been extended on its back, head to the south, the hands crossed on the pelvis or at the sides. The absence of any of the ornamentation or personal jewellery one might have expected in these graves, confirmed the impression of strict discipline and communal living which the first thorough excavations of the ruins themselves also gave. For when, in the following year, the rubble was cleared from the walls, and the main outlines of the building stood out, it was seen that this could be no dwelling house, but some sort of monastery, having large meeting rooms with plaster benches running round the walls, and outside the main building a large water cistern far beyond the needs of an ordinary family. One of the most important of the objects found amongst the ruins was an intact jar of exactly the same shape as those found in the first cave, thus linking quite certainly the cave and the ruins, the Scrolls and the people who had inhabited the Settlement and had been buried in the cemetery. Some evidence of the nature of the destruction of the buildings was found when, in clearing away the surface debris, the excavators came upon a layer of black powder covered with a coating of marl. Careful clearing of the latter revealed the unmistakable remains of charred reeds, and here and there below these, blackened palm trunks. These were clearly the remains of reed roofs laid across palm timbers and plastered with marl in exactly the same fashion as houses are roofed in Jericho to-day. Indeed only a few hundred yards from the ruins the visitor may see a watchman's hut roofed in precisely the same manner. A fire had destroyed the buildings in antiquity, as the charring showed all too clearly, and the presence of iron arrow heads found later in the rooms confirmed the impression of a violent end to the Community.

Gradually the excavator's craft was filling in the outline of the life of these people who had bequeathed to mankind such an amazing legacy of priceless manuscripts. But the second and later seasons were to broaden our knowledge still further; for the Settlement seems to have had a complicated history, whose discernment from the maze of walls and water conduits of the ruins has taxed all the powers of scholarship and resourcefulness of the archaeologists concerned.

With the help of about two hundred and fifty coins found amid the ruins it was possible to sketch out three main periods in the constructional history of Khirbet Qumran, the first two being separated by a period beginning with a violent earthquake. Indeed, the latest excavations make it appear that its history may go back even before the Roman period into the Iron Age, but this cannot be our immediate concern. As far as the Sect is concerned, building seems to have started in or fairly soon after the reign of John Hyrcanus (135–104 B.C.), from which the first important batch of coins found in the ruins come, and the series carry on in an unbroken succession until the time of Herod the Great (37 B.C.–4 B.C.). Only one of his coins has been found, and the series begins again from Herod Archelaus (4 B.C.–A.D. 6) and continues until the second year of the First Revolt (A.D. 68) and the main destruction by fire. There are a handful of coins after this, one of them from Ascalon being countermarked with 'X' on the reverse, probably indicating possession by the Roman Tenth Legion, and the next large batch are of the Second Jewish Revolt of A.D. 132–135. By a stroke of good fortune it is possible to make another pivotal dating in the history of the Settlement, since the earthquake which seems to have brought the first occupational period to an end can be accurately dated. From the historian, Flavius Josephus, writing in the first century of our era, we learn that in the spring of 31 B.C. a terrible earthquake shook Judaea, devastating its towns and killing thousands of men and beasts. It happened in the seventh year of Herod the Great, when he was actively engaged against the Nabateans. The earthquake, we are told, so terrified his men, encamped in the plains of Jericho, that he had difficulty in exhorting them to courage in the face of the enemy. It was most probably this shock which caused the crack in the cistern shown in Plate 27 and which ran right through the adjoining cistern and room leaving a subsidence of 20 inches or so to the east of this line. In the NW. tower, the eastern wall is split, and the lintel of the door between two of the rooms is broken, causing the ceiling of one to collapse. On the walls S. and E. of this room, the plaster is cracked in two lines converging on the SE. corner. Clearly all this damage points to a violent shaking of the earth, and the evidence of the coins would point to the beginning of Herod's reign for its occurrence, which fits well with Josephus' earthquake of 31 B.C. But one question still awaits a definite answer: Did the earthquake drive out the inhabitants or had they already left when it occurred? One can understand their being frightened at the time, and scurrying out of the buildings, but they could easily retire to their caves or tents and come back later to clear up the mess. Yet apparently they did not return for something like thirty years, until after Herod had died. If that king had anything to do with their retirement from Qumran, then they would probably have gone before the earthquake in 31, since he had by then been ruling for seven years. But that raises a difficulty, for if, as now seems probable, this sect is to be identified with a party of the Essenes, Josephus tells us that Herod was favourably inclined towards them because one of their number had once given a favourable prognostication regarding certain of his activities. On the other hand, it is doubtful whether this would have stopped him clearing them out of Qumran if he had felt that their presence on his frontiers was a menace to security.

In any case the Sectarians seem to have returned after his death and cleared out the rubble from the buildings and rebuilt the walls. A trench, sunk on the north side by the excavators, cut through one of the rubbish dumps made at this time, and brought to light whole and broken pottery and a few coins, as well as the rubble of stone and plaster from the broken walls. This second period then lasted until the fall of the monastery in A.D. 68. At this point again we have some welcome confirmatory evidence from Josephus, who tells us that, in the late spring of this year, the emperor Vespasian brought his Tenth Legion down the Jordan Valley to Jericho. Hearing strange stories about the wonderful buoyancy of the Dead Sea he had the hands of several non-swimmers tied behind their backs and threw them into the water. Sure enough they floated, but one hopes for their sakes that they kept their eyes shut against the salt saturated water or they might well have wished they had not. We are told that Vespasian left a garrison at Jericho, and in the following year Titus led the Legion against Jerusalem to raze that city to the ground.

It is possible that the Sectarians of Qumran did not stay to the bitter end, but deposited their precious scrolls against their return and then hastened away before it was too late. Josephus tells us that the Roman approach was heralded by a general panic, when the mass of the population fled into 'those mountainous parts which lay over against Jerusalem'. The presence of the arrow heads among the debris certainly points to some resistance from the buildings, but since the Zealots were certainly active in Masada and En Geddi to the south, it is not impossible that it was they who took over the defence of this strategic position commanding the way to the south and offering a perfect look-out to the head of the Dead Sea. It may have been their defence which the Romans avenged with fire and sword.

The victors did not leave immediately, and the third period in the life of the buildings is marked by a re-utilization of its defence works, the levelling of the debris to some extent, and the division of the larger meeting rooms into small living quarters. They enlarged the bread oven which had been built towards the end of the last Sectarian occupation, and made changes in the water conduits to serve their practical needs of mere physical existence. The large cisterns were no longer used, which points to a much smaller group of inhabitants without the ritualistic requirement for water of the Sect. After a time these too left, and the place remained empty until, in the time of the Second Revolt, the Jewish guerilla forces made use of the monastery's excellent strategic position for a strong point protecting the Dead Sea route to their southern posts. When they too withdrew, the desert took possession of its own, and save for the occasional wandering shepherd none came to break its peace or recall the glories of its past, until Muhammad Adh-Dhib lost his goat one summer's day in 1947.

Now, thanks to the skilful work of Harding and De Vaux and their teams, the visitor can walk again through the rooms and passages of the monastery. It may be of interest to describe in detail some of the more interesting characteristics of the building. The walls stand highest at the NW.

corner which contains the watch tower already mentioned. Here they are some four or five feet thick, and the lower stage contains rooms which communicate with each other but not externally. They give the impression of a closely guarded store-house, or even prison cells. A spiral staircase originally communicated with the upper stage, and its central pillar is still to be seen in one of the lower rooms (pl. 29). On the higher stage of the tower were three rooms with a door to the outside facing south. But this door was accessible only by means of a ladder, or, perhaps, a wooden gallery running along the west wall as far as a staircase, whose remains are visible a few yards to the south. Two open passages surrounding the south and east sides of the tower completed its isolation from the rest of the building. To the south of the tower a block of four or five rooms was probably once covered over, and the most interesting of them is certainly a long rectangular chamber, which may once have been a place of prayer. Unfortunately there was no furniture left in the ruins of the lower storey to tell the tale, apart from the remains of a large reed mat, some seven or eight feet wide, at the southern end of the room. However, above the collapsed ceiling, the remains told a different story. The excavators found a broken structure, having a brick base covered with carefully shaped and smoothed plaster (pl. 32). The pieces were carefully wrapped in cheese cloth, pasted on the outside to give them some rigidity, and transported to the Museum in Jerusalem. There they were patiently reconstructed and found to constitute a narrow table, some seventeen feet long and twenty inches high, and one or two other tables rather shorter in length (pl. 33). These structures were associated with plaster benches which ran round the walls. Also reconstructed was a desk top, divided by a ridge longitudinally into two sections, each with a small basin hollowed out at the top (pl. 34). Two inkwells, one of brass, the other of baked clay, and both containing remains of a carbon ink of the type used on the scrolls (pl. 35), completed the picture. The archaeologists had discovered the very room where many of the fabulous Dead Sea Scrolls had been written. The ink-wells were of a Roman type, examples of which have been found in Egypt and Italy, and are of the 'non-spill' kind still to be seen in our schools in Britain. It seems probable that the bowls in the desk top were used to carry a purifying water into which the hands of the pious scribe would be dipped before commencing work on the Holy Scripture, or perhaps before writing the Divine Name.

To the east of the tower was a complex of rooms with a number of hearths which might well have been the communal kitchen, and later excavations brought to light a large dining-hall, with a pantry attached, containing over a thousand small dishes, neatly stacked in piles on the floor against the walls (pl. 36, 37). The SE. corner of the building was occupied by the two cracked cisterns already mentioned, and, by them, a workshop with the remains of iron tools, and to the north, a latrine made on the well-proved septic tank principles. Surrounded by paving, a collar of pottery gave into a large bell of crude clay which was imbedded into stones down to the marly layer of the terrace, making a small septic tank. There is also nearby a wash place with a large sink, to complete the toilet facilities of the Settlement.

As well as the Scriptorium, other rooms were found with plaster benches round the walls, all pointing to communal use, either for worship or for the council meetings mentioned in the Qumran literature.

The most striking characteristic of the monastery is the number and size of the water cisterns (pl. 30), and the complexity of the conduit systems. The earthquake ruined some, and when, on re-occupation, more were built, the water had to be diverted along new channels. But the maze became so complicated as changes were instituted to satisfy some new need or the pet scheme of an Overseer, that to sort them out has been one of the main difficulties of an already intricate excavation. The water system alone has probably accounted for a reduction of at least a centimetre in Father De Vaux's patriarchal beard, which he is apt to chew in moments of mental stress. On the western side of the monastery the remains of an aqueduct can be seen running back into the *falaise.* If the visitor follows this double line of stones and climbs up some distance to the head of the Wady Qumran, he will come across a tunnel which has been cut out of the rock for several yards, and can crawl through without difficulty until he emerges at the source of the Settlement's water supply.

The cisterns in the Khirbet are well made and carefully plastered, with steps at one end leading down into the water, a characteristic and very necessary feature of Roman cisterns in the area, allowing of the drawing of water from whatever level it may be. The water thus collected from the head of the Wady would have to last nine or ten months of the year, so that it is not surprising that so much was required for a community of probably about five hundred souls. Besides that necessary for the sustaining of life, water purification rites played a large part in their religious devotions, necessitating an enlarged supply. Whether the cisterns were ever used as baptistries seems doubtful, and it is more likely that the sectarians would have preferred the running water of the Jordan with its ancient associations, or even of 'Ain Feshkha to the south, to the static tanks in the Settlement. But it is a question which cannot be resolved for certain either way at present.

The Combing of the Cliffs

As was mentioned in Chapter Two, an expedition was launched in the spring of 1952 to take the initiative from the Ta'amireh and to search the cliffs behind the Settlement for a distance of five miles, its centre being the Khirbet. It was a joint venture again, this time of Father De Vaux and his team from the French School, and Dr W. Reed with a party from the American School. Between 10 and 29 March the party of seven archaeologists, each in charge of a gang of three or four Bedouin, explored every nook and cranny of the hills behind the Settlement. Just what that involves can only be fully appreciated by a visit to the spot, but perhaps the plates of the area (26, 38) might give some idea. The limestone of the crags lends itself particularly easily to fissures and clefts which could make ideal hiding places. No less than two hundred and thirty unfruitful soundings were made, and many of them perched high in the cliff sides, taking hours of stiff climbing to reach, let alone excavate. Lest it be imagined that the work entailed no more than peering in to see if there were any scroll jars, let the reader be assured that before any cave could be pronounced sterile, every scrap of dust and loose rock had to be sifted through the finger tips, lest any precious fragments be missed. Very often the excavators would have to go down several inches before reaching virgin rock beneath, and to concentrate on this work, when one's eyes and ears and throat are clogged with the irritating dust, and the temperature rising to the hundred mark, takes a great deal of will power. Then, when that cave was explored, the party would have to move on to another, perhaps hundreds of feet above or below, and start afresh. However, thirty-seven caves or holes in the rock were found to contain pottery or other remains of human habitation, and twenty-five of these held pottery identical with that found in the first cave and the Settlement, thus proving beyond doubt that they were used by the same people at the same time. The sizes and general shape of the caves varied a great deal. Some were large and open, and having been used by shepherds over the centuries, were consequently archaeologically poor. Others were low and narrow, or mere cracks in the rocks, so that, although pottery and the like was found in them, it is doubtful whether they were ever used for habitation, but probably only for storage. It was not therefore surprising to find that a great many sherds from characteristic Qumran storage jars were found there, along with articles of day-to-day use like cooking pots, juglets, bowls, and lamps. It appears, then, that the Sectarians had lived outside many of these caves, using them only for storage, whilst they themselves dwelt in huts or tents. Indeed, in one crevice, along with the usual hoard of pottery, were found several forked sticks, almost certainly tent poles. That they belonged to the same period as the pottery was certain, since the entrance to the crevice had been blocked in antiquity with heavy stones.

One significant negative feature of the search was the complete absence of money in the caves. This seemed to De Vaux to point to a communistic mode of living, where all financial transactions were carried out by the central authority of the Sect, and all wealth put into a common pool. As we shall see, the documents confirm this view, and make this surrender of all personal wealth a necessary condition of full membership of the Community.

The most exciting discovery of the expedition occurred on 14 March when the only scroll cave found, later numbered Three, was discovered. It is some way north of the first cave and near the limit of the explored area. The roof had fallen in long ago, with the result that very few leather fragments were found, though the remains of forty jars and twenty-six lids testified to the possibility of there having once been a large library stored there. The disappointment of the excavators, however, was amply compensated for by the discovery, hard up against the wall of the cave near the entrance, of a rolled-up copper strip, broken across at an inner riveting, and rolled like this into two separate 'scrolls'. They once formed a continuous plate of metal about 8 feet long and 12 inches wide. In the centre of the larger of the two rolls can be seen the traces of further riveting, so that originally there had been three sheets. Although the metal had by now become completely oxidized, from the outside could be seen heavy indenting of Hebrew or Aramaic letters, so that if only the rolls could be opened or cut safely, it seemed to the excavators that some important message might emerge. They were taken in 1955 to Manchester, and there, in the laboratories of the College of Technology of that city, the scroll was successfully cut into strips, and its contents deciphered by the author (Appendix IV).

After three weeks the team and even the Bedouin were

becoming very exhausted and the search had to be brought to an end. Certainly there are still caves in the area which have not yet been explored. Doubtless there are some whose existence is hidden by a fall of rock obscuring their entrances, and it is by no means improbable that the Bedouin will find another scroll cave in the vicinity, although if they do, we can only pray that by then there will have been formed a central fund from which the material can be bought quickly without all the heart-breaking and time-consuming begging which has had such a dispiriting effect on previous finds.

CHAPTER SIX

THE ORIGIN OF THE SECT

WE saw from the last chapter that the archaeological evidence provides an historical framework for the Qumran Sect, with a beginning in or soon after the reign of John Hyrcanus (135–104 B.C.), and a violent end shortly before the destruction of Jerusalem in A.D. 70. Within that framework we are now able to fill out the story with more detail, thanks to internal documentary evidence. Of most importance from this point of view are certain biblical commentaries found in the Qumran library. But it should be understood that these commentaries are very different from the objective expositions of biblical books which we find on our library shelves to-day. In the first place, the Qumran commentator is not at all interested in the historical and social context of the biblical prophecy. For him, every word of Scripture was pregnant with meaning for his own day, and it is in its contemporary relevance that the interpreter is interested. In the process of arriving at its import for his time, nothing is barred to the commentator: any twisting of the meanings of words, reference to variant traditions known to the author although not included in the text before him, word plays, and even rewriting the passage to suit his interpretation, all is legitimate to the Qumran writer who is himself fired with the spirit of prophecy. This 'eschatalogical knowledge', by which the signs of the times could be interpreted in the light of ancient prophecy, was a special divine gift, possessed by the Qumran writers as by Jesus and Paul, and, indeed, the light thrown by these Qumran commentaries on the treatment by New Testament writers of Scripture texts is worth looking at in a later chapter. But to us, seeking first-hand knowledge of the history of the Sect, these references by Qumran authors to contemporary events, in which they saw the signs of the coming of the end of the age, and the new era, can, carefully treated, be most valuable. I say carefully treated, for our authors, as one suspects with certain New Testament writers, are not above changing the events to suit the prophecy, as well as the words of prophecy to suit the events. Furthermore, a convention of the Sect is to use for the most part biblical pseudonyms in place of proper names at any rate in their religious documents. Thus the Roman forces, whose unassailable might made such an impression on their countrymen when they swept through the country in the first century B.C., were referred to as the *Kittîm*, originally applied in the Bible to the inhabitants of Cyprus. The Sect's own leader was called the *Teacher of Righteousness*, although his actual name, real or assumed, seems to have been Zadok. Themselves they called the *Sons of Zadok*, which probably had as much reference to Ezekiel xl. 46 as to the name of their leader.

The Community believed, as presumably the Teacher had himself said, that he had received a special commission from God to gather certain of the Jerusalem priests together and take them into the desert, as a closely knit community of the faithful, there to remain, pure and undefiled, during the present period of apostasy until the end of the age and the coming of the Kingdom of God. Then he and his band would form the nucleus of the new Israel, and the millennium would have dawned for all mankind. There is no doubt that the spirit of unity which shines through the writings of the Sect, and the strictness of their self-imposed discipline, points to the early influence of a very strong personality, whose death soon after the formation of the Sect could not affect the basic order and firm expectations and doctrines of the Community.

There are several references to the persecution of the Teacher at the hands of another oft-recurring figure, the *Wicked Priest*. He is the arch-villain of the drama, and to him is referred any wicked person spoken of in biblical prophecy. In a particularly important commentary on the book of

Nahum, it seems to be this person who is referred to under the pseudonym *The Lion of Wrath*, and, thanks to the added mention of certain recognizable historical events, it is not difficult to identify this figure with the Jewish priest-king, Alexander Jannaeus, who reigned from 104 to 78 B.C. Indeed, long before the recovery of this commentary, many scholars had noted how well this tyrant fitted the characteristics of the Sect's persecutor, and the additional evidence seems to make the identification certain. Another commentary, this time on the book of Habakkuk, tells us that he persecuted the Teacher 'in the House of his exile', presumably Qumran, 'on the day of Atonement', and from this and other references we can now draw up a fairly clear picture of the train of events leading up to the formation of the Sect and execution of the Teacher.

It will be remembered that the Maccabean Revolt of 168 B.C., graphically described for us in the First Book of Maccabees, arose out of the determination of Antiochus Epiphanes, the Greek ruler, to impose a Hellenistic civilization on the culturally backward Jews. He was but following out the intentions of his predecessor, Alexander the Great, whose dream was to create an empire, bound not so much by the power of the sword as by the coherence of a common culture. Although Antiochus had a measure of success in Judaea, among a 'free-thinking' section of the priesthood, he found, to his disgust, that there was a hard core of obstinate priests and people who refused to abandon the faith of their forefathers and be 'westernized'. Severe punitive measures merely brought the matter to a head, and, in the inevitable revolt which followed, the Jewish rebels won a series of brilliant victories under the leadership of the Maccabean family. In 165 B.C., they were able to rededicate a cleansed Temple in Jerusalem, and throw out the heathen altar with which Antiochus had most horribly defiled the Temple three years previously. There was naturally much rejoicing, and, indeed, the event is celebrated by Jewry to this day, but not all sections of the people were so pleased. Besides those who hankered after the new culture, there was still a hard core of orthodox Jews, led by a section of the priesthood, who saw the Maccabean victories at the best as 'a little help', as the book of Daniel calls them, a slight palliative for a sickness which went much deeper than mere victories on the field of battle could hope to assuage. For these people, the persecutions of Antiochus were merely just punishment meted out by God to His people for their neglect of His Law, and the breaking of His divine Covenant, made centuries before with Moses. What God required from the Jews was not the shattering of a foreign yoke, but the breaking of their own hearts in true repentance; not the building of a political kingdom under a war leader, but the formation of a theocratic community, ruled by a pious and God-fearing priest, a spiritual shepherd of his people. Many of these pious folk had fled before 168, believing it better to die of starvation in the desert than to deny their God amidst the flesh-pots of Jerusalem. When pursued by their enemies, they had submitted to death in their hundreds rather than take up arms to defend themselves on the Sabbath. The Maccabees had seen, however, that this was no way to fight a war, and had persuaded some, at least, to abandon their principles for the time being and sacrifice all to the immediate end of winning their political independence. But not all were so tempted, and many remained true to their Law, earning the name of the Pious Ones, or *Hasidim*. Out of this group we can almost certainly trace the origins of the *Essenes*, and the *Pharisees*.

The doubts of the Hasidim were soon justified by events. The Maccabean House, or Hasmoneans, were awarded the High Priesthood of Israel, although their claim to this high office was, to say the least, tenuous. This was no mere religious archbishopric, but a divine office given by God to a priest of His choosing, by which he might in all matters govern the Chosen People. He was the spiritual and temporal head of the nation, supreme arbiter in matters of faith and conduct, and must himself fulfil certain stringent conditions of race and purity before he could take office. In the days of the hated Antiochus, the position had been thrown open to the highest bidder, following on the banishment of the pious Onias III, but it was little better now to hand it over into the bloody hands of a warrior chieftain.

Taking the fullest advantage of the weakness of their Seleucid foes, the Hasmonean House greatly expanded the territory of their Jewish kingdom, and then took to themselves the title of King as well as High Priest. This was another step in the rising consternation of the orthodox priests and their followers, and matters reached a head one day during the Feast of Tabernacles, when they beheld the most hated of all these warrior priest-kings, Alexander Jannaeus, offering the sacred sacrifice at the Temple altar. Not only were his hands red with the blood of countless battles, but they believed he had no right to his high office since he was but the son of a slave woman, and thus not of pure descent. We are told that the people screamed abuse at him, and began throwing the citron fruits they carried as part of the celebrations. Jannaeus was not the man to take this lightly, and he set his mercenary troops on to his own people, massacring several thousands. We should not be far wrong if we saw the hand of the Qumran Teacher behind these events, for one of the scrolls looks forward to the time when 'bastards and sons of strangers' should never again set foot in the restored Temple of the New Jerusalem. In any case, it seems most probable that, at this time, the Teacher gathered together some of the faithful priests of the Holy City and fled to the deserts of Qumran. There they began their exile from mankind, which would end only when God saw fit to vindicate His faithful and bring in His Kingdom. The presence of dozens of cooking pots, buried near the Monastery walls, and containing the remains of presumably sacred meals, together with suggestive references in the Sect's literature, seems to suggest that at Qumran the fugitives built for themselves a new, temporary sanctuary, where sacrifices could be offered up by the pure hands of their Teacher, now regarded as the true High Priest of Israel.

This was certainly to be his title when he arose to be the

priestly Messiah of Israel, and if, indeed, he took it at this time, it could only have been interpreted as a deliberate attempt to overthrow the authority of Jannaeus. There was no room in Israel for two High Priests, and the sacred office carried with it the secular rule of the nation. The Teacher is hardly likely to have been so much interested in this, but to Jannaeus his action would have been taken as a political rebellion, and as such, meriting a particularly dreadful punishment which he had learnt from his Gentile mercenaries. This was execution by crucifixion, or the hanging of a man alive from a stake until he died of starvation and exposure. Denied the decency of burial, the body was allowed to hang there until it rotted, an idea most abhorrent to every Jew. That Jannaeus allowed this atrocity to be practised in his reign we learn from an incident recorded by the ancient historian Josephus. Following the massacre in Jerusalem, Alexander went off to fight more wars with his neighbours, and was heavily defeated by the Nabatean king, Obedas. He barely escaped with his life, and just managed to struggle back to Jerusalem, only to find that the Pharisees had taken this opportunity offered by his weakness to make open rebellion against him. After six years of civil war, they took the unwise step of seeking foreign aid, in the person of the Greek monarch, Demetrius III, Eucaerus. He arrived with an army and met the malcontents at Shechem, and together they dealt Alexander a crushing blow. But then Josephus tells us that strangely enough many of the rebels changed sides and joined Jannaeus' defeated army. Light on this event is, however, cast by a Qumran commentary on Nahum, which tells us that Demetrius had tried to enter Jerusalem. This, of course, was the natural step for a victorious commander to have taken, but whilst it was one thing having a foreigner fight one's battles, it was another having him tread the sacred courts of the Holy City itself. So many of his supporters deserted him, choosing the lesser of two evils, and Demetrius was obliged to retire to Damascus. Alexander then set about rounding up those who had remained with his enemies, and, dragging them forth from their places of refuge, turned them over to his mercenaries to be crucified. We are told that the stakes were erected on the terrace below the palace, so that Jannaeus could enjoy the spectacle whilst carousing with his harem. He also commanded that the wives and children of the wretched victims should be massacred before their dying eyes.

This practice of crucifying his political enemies is credited to the Lion of Wrath in the Nahum Commentary, and it further comments that this was never before done in Israel, being essentially a foreign punishment. One might surmise that the Sectarians had particular cause to recall this activity of Jannaeus, since their Master had suffered the same cruel death, the recognized punishment of a rebel.

The Habakkuk Commentary makes a point of its being the Day of Atonement when the Wicked Priest confronted the Master and his followers in the 'house of their exile'. This might imply, if what I have said about the temporary sanctuary at Qumran is correct, that the Master was even then officiating at the altar when Jannaeus appeared. In any case, the scene as these two priests faced one another must have been dramatic enough. The one, haughty and proud, scarred by the wounds of many battles, and the ravaging of a lifetime of greed and lechery, the other, white-robed and saintly, gazing scornfully on his enemy, secure in his simple trust in God and the hope of resurrection to eternal life. Would that those disciples, who perhaps watched the scene from the crags above the Monastery, had included a Mark or Luke. But connected narratives of this type have no place in Qumran literature.

CHAPTER SEVEN

THE LIFE AND DISCIPLINE OF THE SECT

FOR our information about the rules of initiation and conduct of the Sect we are mainly dependent on the *Damascus Document,* so-called because it describes the place of exile of the Sect figuratively as 'Damascus' after Amos v.27, and, probably, Zechariah ix.1, and an almost complete work found in the Qumran library called *The Rule for all the Congregation of Israel in the Last Days,* or more popularly nowadays, since its translation by the American scholars, *The Manual of Discipline* (pl. 13). Both the *Manual* and the *Damascus Document* talk of another handbook which had to be known perfectly by the leaders of the Sect and taught to the younger members, called the Book of Hagī (or Hagū). So far no identifiable remains of this work have appeared, but it is possible that we have it without knowing, since, apart from possible quotations in the *Manual* and the *Damascus Document,* the book is quite unknown.

The Sect knew itself primarily as the 'Covenant' (*bĕrīth*), and specifically as the 'New Covenant' (*bĕrīth ḥădāshah*). Other names were the 'Congregation' (*'ēdah*), 'Assembly' (*qahal*), 'Party' (*'ēṣah,* sometimes also meaning 'Council'), and 'Community' (*yaḥad*), a word conveying the idea of 'unity', and these last two are often combined into 'Party of the Community' (*'ēṣath ha-yaḥad*). This idea of unity lay very close to the heart of the Sect, and the same word *yaḥad* is used very often adverbially meaning 'in common'. Thus they shared all the necessities of life, spiritual as well as material:

> For everything shall be (held) in common, Truth and fair humility, and faithful love, and just consideration for one's fellow in the holy Council . . .

There was no place for the egoist in such a gathering:

> No man shall walk in the stubbornness of his heart to err after his own will, eyes and purpose.

They took their meals communally, and sang their praises to God together, and in joint session held their deliberate councils. When one became a full member of the Sect, he 'mixed' his worldly possessions in the common pool, and he received back only the necessities of life. However, it should not be thought that this was an egalitarian society, where each man was as good as his fellow. We have frequent mention of their 'ranks', and according to their respective status in the society was their order of seating in the deliberative assemblies, of their speaking, and in fact of practically every communal activity. And in everything the priests had precedence. It is true that in a special sense the whole Community saw themselves as a joint priesthood,

> an eternal planting, a holy house of Israel, an assembly of supreme holiness for Aaron . . .

but beginning as a priestly society, founded by a priestly Teacher, it was the priestly element which held the casting vote in matters of moment concerning the whole of the Community. In any group of ten persons, one had to be a priest, and the laymen had to sit before him according to their rank. Nevertheless, the government of the Community seems to have been run on democratic grounds in that, with certain safeguards, any member could speak, and all could vote. The priesthood formed a kind of Second Chamber, and their decision was regarded as divinely inspired, and was revealed by a 'casting of the lot', probably some oracular device such as the biblical Urim and Thummim, which is actually mentioned and described to some extent in one of their documents.

That women and children had some place in the Community, as ideally constituted, is shown by the heading of the *Manual*:

> when they come they will gather together all the arrivals, women and children, and will recite (in their ears) all the statutes of the Covenant.

Then, in discussing the upbringing of boys, it lays down that a lad may not take a woman to wife until he is twenty, by which time he should know the difference between good and evil. Then he must realize the responsibilities involved, for, from that time, the wife may witness against him in process of law and may take part in the deciding of the issue. More material evidence of the presence of women at Qumran has been the discovery of female skeletons in the cemetery. Furthermore, some of the rules of the *Damascus Document* seem to have been formulated with a view to family life and speak of orphans and unmarried women requiring help.

The rules for the conducting of a session of the Congregation would delight the heart of many a committee chairman.

> Every man (will be placed) according to his rank. First the priests will sit down, second the elders and then the remainder of all the people according to their respective ranks. In this order shall they be asked concerning a decision or any counsel or matter which shall concern the Many, and each man shall recount what he knows to the Council of the Community. Let no man interrupt his fellow whilst he is speaking, and let no man jump his assigned position to speak. The man who is asked to do so shall speak in his turn. And in a session of the Many, let no man say anything displeasing to the majority or which is not by direction of the Overseer. If any man who is not in the position of Interlocutor of the Many wishes to speak, let him rise to his feet and say, 'I have something to say to the Many'. If they call him, he shall speak.

It may be added that any infringement of this almost unbelievable good order was severely punished.

The executive head of the Party seems to have been a special Council of twelve men and three priests. Overseers are the executive officers of the Community, regulating the work, keeping accounts, and acting as chairmen to these ideal general meetings. Another officer, whose task it was to act as examiner of those applying for membership, is called the Inspector (*pāqīd*). Of the judges of the Congregation, four were priests and six laymen, all well versed in the

Book of Hagī and the Law of Moses, and none must be younger than twenty-five or older than sixty.

Here is a summary of the penal code as given in the *Manual.* Exclusion from the 'Purity of the Many' means a temporary or permanent excommunication from full initiation, so that the offender is reduced, as it were, to the ranks, being of no higher status than that of a probationer. 'Fining' means a deprivation of rations, serious enough in a Community which would in any case be living on the bare necessities of life.

For deliberate lying in the matter of personal possessions – exclusion from the Purity of the Many for one year, and one quarter rations.

Bearing a grudge unjustly against one's fellow – six months (a later hand has written above the line 'one year'), and taking personal vengeance – the same.

Foolish speech – three months.

Interrupting another person speaking – ten days.

Sleeping during a session of the Many – thirty days.

Leaving a session without permission or good reason, up to three times in a single session – ten days.

Unnecessary self-exposure – six months.

Indecent exposure during bodily movement – thirty days.

Spitting during a session of the Many – thirty days.

Foolish laughter – thirty days.

Slandering one's fellow – exclusion for one year; slandering the Many – banishment for ever.

Murmuring against the institution of the Community – banishment for ever; against one's fellow – six months.

A man who is so overawed by the institution of the Community as to betray the truth and walk obstinately alone, and yet he returns – two years. In the first he will not touch the Purity of the Many, and in the second he will not approach the Banquet of the Many but shall take his place after all the others. When his two years are completed, his case will be investigated and if they admit him, he will be enrolled according to his rank, and may therefore be consulted in judgement. A veteran of more than ten years, however, who shall similarly default, shall return no more, and

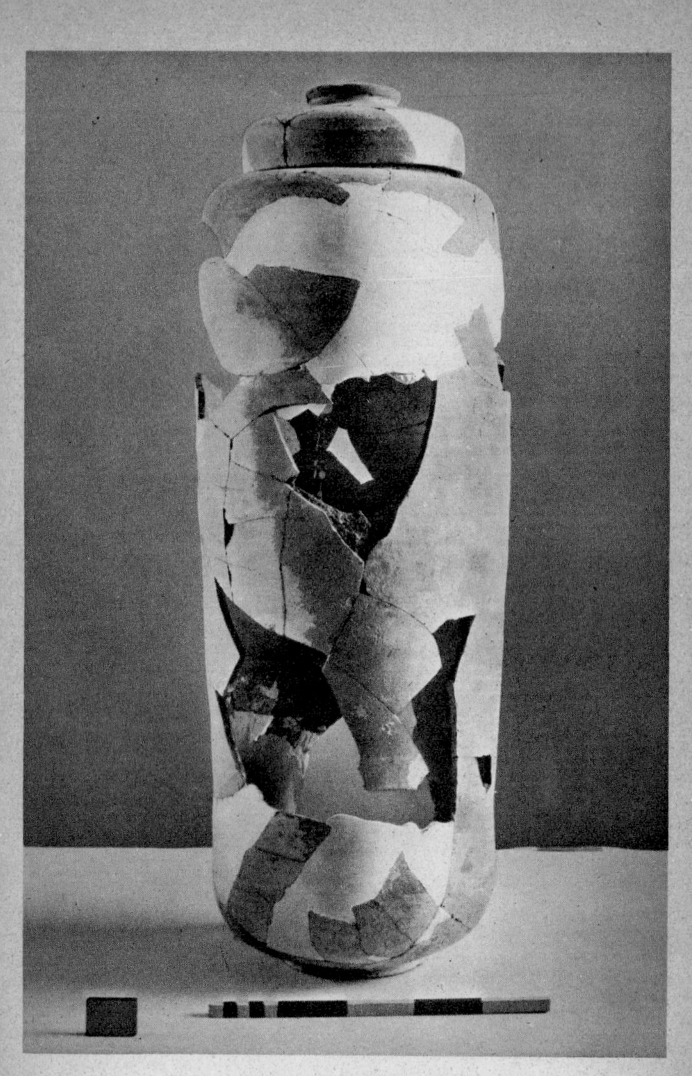

1. A reconstructed Scroll jar from Cave One

2. Muhammad's Cave (One)

3. Kando and George

4. Caves in the Wady Murabba'at (One & Two)

5. Inside Cave One, Murabba'at

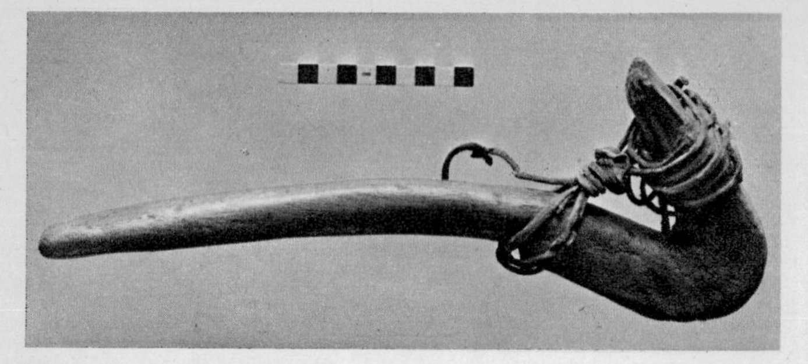

6. A chalcolithic wooden adze handle, with leather thongs attached, from a Murabba'at cave (*c.* 4000 B.C.)

7. A papyrus letter from Murabba'at, written by the leader of the Second Jewish Revolt (A.D. 132–135), Simon ben Kosebah (Kochebah)

8. Climbing to Cave Two

9. Wady Qumran, the Monastery and the Dead Sea to the Jordan inlet, taken from the vicinity of Cave Six

10. Cave Three: home of the Copper Scroll

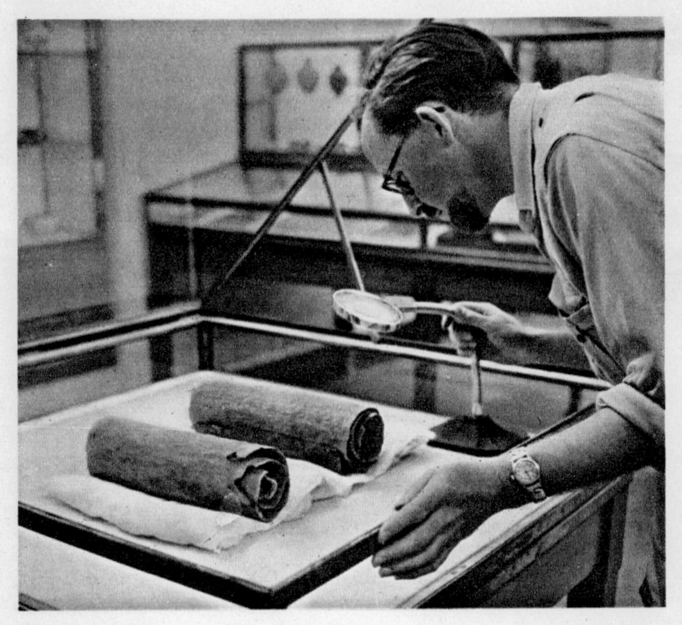

11. The Copper Scroll on view in the Palestine Archaeological Museum before opening

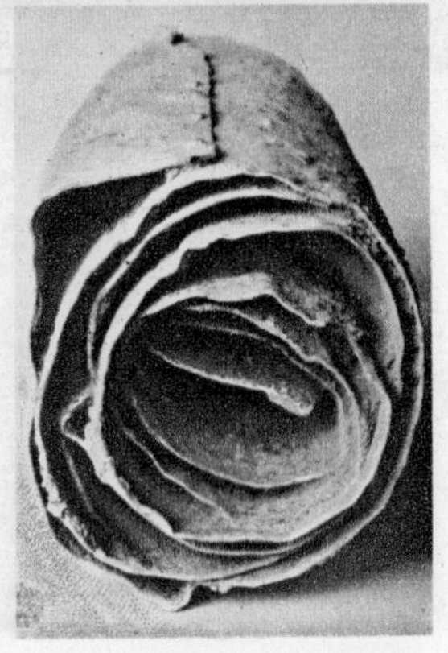

12. The bottom edge of the larger of the copper strips

13. The title page of the 'Manual of Discipline'

14. Cave Four

15. Caves Four and Five

16. Some members of the 'Scrollery' team; John Strugnell, the author, Father Skehan, Claus Hunzinger, and Father Milik

17. Frank Cross at work in the 'Scrollery' on some Fourth-Cave biblical fragments

18. Scroll fragments as they are received from the Bedouin

19. Joins in biblical fragments from the Fourth Cave

20. The 'Scrollery'

21. Part of a scroll of Samuel from the Fourth Cave: this piece is made up of 27 fragments

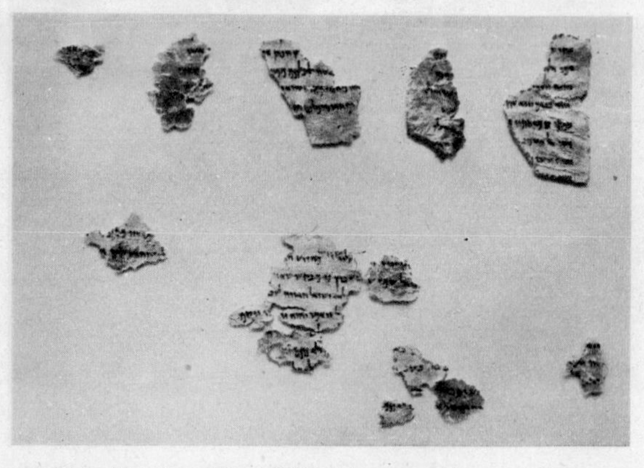

22. Probably the oldest biblical document known: fragments from a third-century B.C. scroll of Samuel

23. Fragments of a Fourth-Cave scroll of Exodus, written in the old, protohebraic ('Phoenician-type') script

24. Part of a commentary on Psalm 37

25. The walls of the Qumran Monastery

26. South across the Monastery, after the first short season's excavations

27. The steps of a monastery cistern, cracked probably by the earthquake of 31 B.C.

28. Father De Vaux, Father Milik, and Gerald Lankester Harding

29. The North-western tower of the Qumran Monastery

30. A large and well-preserved cistern of the Qumran Monastery

31. The monastery pottery kiln

32. The Scriptorium of the Monastery, with remains of the plaster benches

33. The reconstructed writing tables and benches from the Scriptorium

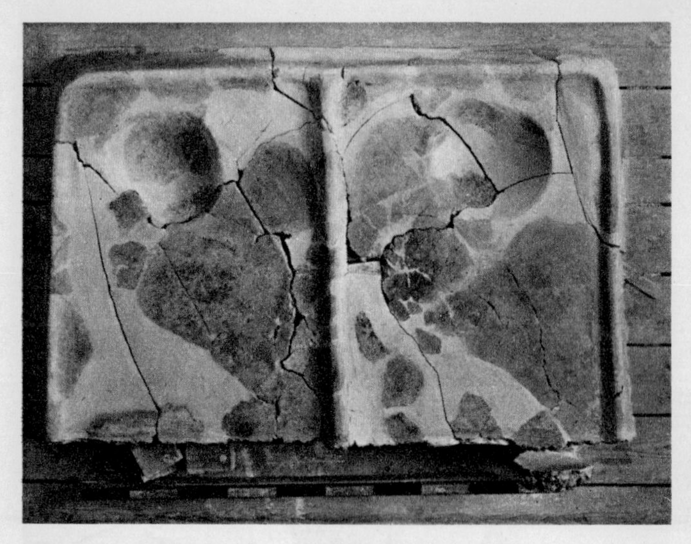

34. Writing tables from the Scriptorium

35. Scriptorium ink-wells of terra-cotta and bronze

36. The Monastery dining-hall

37. Domestic crockery preserved in a corner of the pantry

38. The pass above Qumran to the Buqeia'

39. A papyrus letter from the administrators of Bēth Māshekô, found at Murabba'at

40. Torn fragments from a scroll of Exodus, found in a Murabba'at cave

41. A Murabba'at marriage contract, written in a hitherto unknown Hebrew cursive script

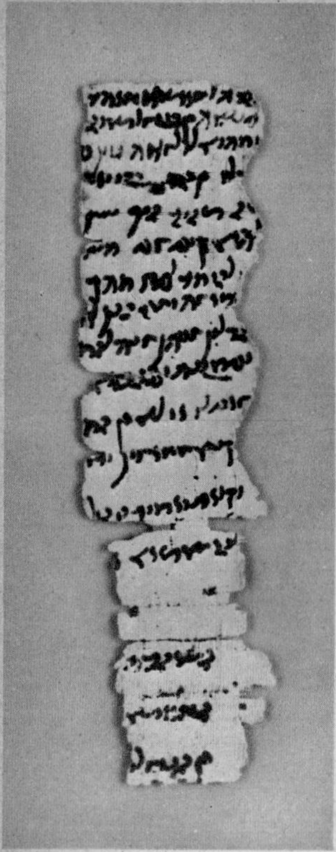

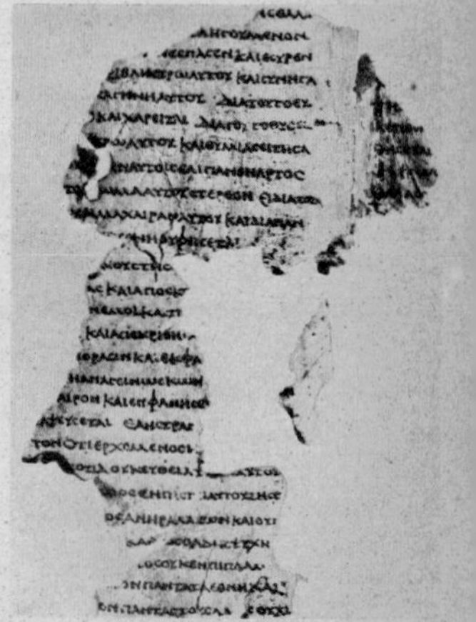

42. Part of a scroll of a Greek translation of the Minor Prophets, from an unknown source

anybody associating with such a person will suffer the same fate.

Initiation

The *Manual* lays down three stages through which the initiate must pass. The first, of unspecified period, is a matter of becoming acquainted with the spirit and practices of the Sect and is preceded by an examination by the Inspector of his motives and general outlook. At the conclusion of this stage, the Many debate his case and may, if satisfied, admit him to the next stage, or alternatively, can reject him altogether. If promoted, he will then pass into the Party of the Community, but without touching the Purity of the Many. At the end of a further year, a general session of the Community will deliberate on his suitability for further promotion and if favourably inclined, may admit him to the last stage, which again will last one year. In this last stage he will hand over to the Overseer all his worldly wealth, and it will be marked to his credit but not yet 'mixed' in with the common pool. He is still excluded from the Messianic Banquet, but is now apparently admitted to the Purity of the Many. If, on his completion of this stage, he is adjudged fit to enter full membership, he is enrolled and assigned a rank amongst brethren. Now, and only now, may he take his share in the Community decisions, be asked for his counsel, and permitted to pool his possessions with the Sect's. He has now entered the Covenant before God,

> to do all that He has commanded, and to remain constant in following Him even in the face of terror, fright, or ordeal which may face him during the dominion of Belial.

At the initiation ceremony the priests and the Levites pronounce their blessings praising 'the God of deliverances and all His deeds of faithfulness', and all the members say 'Amen! Amen!'. Then follows a recitation of the wondrous works of God, His compassionate works of grace towards Israel, whilst the Levites recount the rebelliousness of the people and their sin under the dominion of Belial. Then those entering the Covenant make a general confession:

> We have been perverse [. . .], we have done wickedly, we and our forefathers before us, walking [. . .] truth. But [God] is righteous, [who has executed] His judgements upon us and upon our fathers; and His faithful mercies he has bestowed upon us from everlasting to everlasting.

Following this, the priests bless the 'men of God's lot, who walk perfectly in all His ways,' and say:

> May He bless thee with every good: may He keep thee from all evil, and illumine thy heart with the knowledge of life, and favour thee with eternal wisdom. And may He lift up the face of His sure mercies upon you to everlasting peace.

The Levites then take up their curses upon the men of Belial's party, condemn them to eternal fire, and proceed to give a solemn warning to those who would enter this sacred Covenant that, should they prove unfaithful to it,

> their lot will be placed in the midst of the eternally accursed.

Again the new members respond with the two-fold Amen. This, we may be sure, is the service for reception of new members, but we actually meet it in the *Manual* as the annual Covenant service, where the membership of each initiate is renewed by this service of self-dedication every year, 'all the days of the dominion of Belial', in the order of priests, Levites, and then the people, according to their respective ranks. Thus the Community is kept constantly aware of its blessings and responsibilities and the ever present struggle between the ultimate rule or kingdom of God and the temporary dominion of Belial.

This rite of initiation into the full membership of the Community was probably accompanied by an initial baptism ceremony. Whether or not they used the great cisterns at the Qumran Settlement for this purpose is still open to question, as has been said in Chapter Five. Certainly this would accord with the injunction of the *Damascus Document* that no man shall bathe in water of less depth than that required to cover a person, but whether this ruling had relevance to baptismal ceremonies is not clear. It seems more probable in some ways that the Sect would prefer the traditional running water of the Jordan river not so far away, or nearer still the clear waters of 'Ain Feshkha, though these would only 'cover a man' if he were lying down. We know very little about the actual baptism ceremony, although some fragments from the Fourth Cave tell us something about the benedictions used at this rite. Once a person had been admitted to the Purity of the Many he could be baptized in the same water as other full members, but the Sect was careful that no novitiate or non-member was allowed to touch this water, nor any of his possessions, since he was ritually 'unclean':

> Let him (the 'sinner') not enter the water to come into touch with the purity of the holy men. For such shall not be cleansed until they have repented of their wickedness; for uncleanness is on all transgressors of His word.

Salvation could come to the Qumran Covenanter only by complete separation of himself and his possessions from the world. This was not prompted by any smug self-righteousness on his part, but because he sincerely believed that pollution from the non-purified world meant the risk of contact with the dominion of Belial or the Devil, which might compromise the constant battle he was fighting within himself against the powers of evil. We shall have more to say on this matter when discussing the theology of the Sect, but the same idea prompted their strict disciplinary measures against any defaulting member on what might seem to us trivial faults. To the Sect, the slightest falling away from their very high standards of conduct and ritual purity meant that the member responsible had been brought into the power of the Devil, even though only for a fleeting moment of weakness, but yet in that time had proved himself a weak link in the chain of their defence against the dominion of Belial. Once let the powers of evil get a hold on a man, and he might prove a source of added temptation to other brethren, who must at all costs be protected in this critical time preceding the end of the present world order. Thus the initiate

> will not unite himself with him in his work or his wealth lest he cause him to incur the guilt of transgression: for he must keep far from him in every matter . . . for all who are not reckoned in His Covenant are to be separated, they and all their possessions, and the holy man is not to rely on vain works, for vain are all those who know not His Covenant.

For this reason the rules for initiation are very exacting. This was no missionary Sect, going out into the world looking for members. People who desired the hard and pure life of the Covenanters with its promised blessings of the messianic age came to them and devoted themselves entirely to the cause, withholding nothing. If they came merely because they had suffered disappointments in life or had personal troubles or the like, the chances were that they would soon tire of the tremendous sacrifices demanded of the Sectarian, and fall by the wayside. Such people had to be rooted out before they came near the Purity of full members, hence the long and searching probation. One cannot doubt that at this stage many were turned away, and few reached the full initiation.

The Daily Life of the Covenanter

There is little in the literature so far recovered from Qumran which tells as much about the secular activities of the Covenanter, but a certain amount can be reconstructed from the excavations of the Khirbet. There were certainly the usual domestic tasks to perform, such as cleaning the communal rooms and kitchens, sweeping the plaster floors, raking over those of beaten earth. Some would work in the pottery workshops, preparing the clay, turning the vessels on the wheel, or firing the fashioned jars. The kitchen ovens have been found where the cooks prepared the communal meals, and the pantry where the simple crockery was stacked for the use of the Sectarians in the long dining-hall next door. Continual attention must have been given to building repairs and alterations, and in the winter the water conduits would need to be kept clear of mud and other blockages preventing the desperately needed supply to the cisterns. No doubt the repair of the aqueduct itself was an annual task round about October after eight or nine months of summer drought. At this time the empty cisterns would be examined for cracks in the plaster which, if not repaired in time, would allow the precious water to seep away into the ground. The simple reed and marl roofs would require attention after the summer's sun, if they were to withstand the heavy winter showers. And all through the year the shepherds and goatherds tended their flocks in the vicinity and particularly by the fresh vegetation of the 'Ain Feshkha, where doubtless simple farming also was carried on by the members to provide food for their Community.

From the Scriptorium would come the steady scratching of pens, as the scribes copied their precious scrolls, and nearby their fellows prepared the inks and skins for their use. Perhaps the women of the Community would be weaving the flaxen cloths for wrapping scrolls for storage, and either in the Settlement or in the caves a librarian was at his task of sorting and classifying the texts.

And all the time, day and night, came the chant of the recited Law or the hymns of thanksgiving. The duty of studying the Mosaic Law was taken very seriously. God's command to Joshua that

> this book of the Law shall not depart out of thy mouth, but thou shalt meditate therein day and night . . .

was carried out to the letter by the Community:

> Let the Many keep awake in community a third of all the nights in the year in order to read aloud from the Book and to expound Judgement and to sing blessings altogether.

Here is one of the hymns they sang, as recovered from their scroll of Thanksgiving Psalms:

I thank thee, O Lord,
That thou hast tied my soul in the bundle of life
and fenced me about from all the snares of the Pit.
Ruthless men have sought my life,
because I hold fast to thy Covenant.
But they are an empty crowd, a tribe of Belial,
failing to see that in thee is my foothold:
that thou, with thy mercy, wilt deliver my soul,
for my footsteps are of thine ordering.

Even their striving against me comes from thee,
that thou mayest be glorified in thy condemnation
of the wicked,
and that thou mayest be magnified in me before men,
for I stand by thy grace.
And I said, Warriors are encamped against me;
they surround me with every warlike weapon,
and shower down arrows without relief.
The spearhead flashes like a forest fire,
the din of their shouting roars like the flood,
like a storm driving havoc before it . . .

But as for me, when my heart dissolveth like water,
then my soul takes strength from thy Covenant;
and the net they prepared to catch me
will entangle their own feet;
and the traps they set for my soul,
will cause their downfall.

And out of their midst I will bless thy name.

The following are extracts from other hymns of the collection, chosen mainly from the point of view of their theological interest.

I thank thee, O Lord,
that thou hast redeemed my soul from the Pit
and hast raised me from Hell's Abaddon to the
Everlasting Height.

And I shall walk in the boundless plains,
and know that there will be a final gathering
for those whom thou hast created from clay
to join an eternal Council.
Thou hast purified the perverted from the great transgression
to stand alongside the army of saints,
and to enter the throng of the angels of heaven.
And thou hast allotted to men an everlasting
portion with the spirits of knowledge,
to praise thy name in the Community,
and to recount thy wonders before all thy Creation . . .

And I am dust and ashes;
What shall I purpose without thy good pleasure,
and what shall I devise without thy good will?
How shall I be strong unless thou supportest me,
and how shall I have wisdom unless thou createst
it for me?
And how shall I speak but thou dost open my mouth,
and how shall I answer but thou dost give me wisdom?

Behold, thou art the prince of gods (*'ēlīm*),
King of the glorious ones, and Lord of every spirit,
Ruler of all Creation, and apart from thee
nothing was made.
Nothing is known without thy good will, and there is none
save thee.
There is none beside thee in strength,
and none before thee in glory,
and to thy greatness there is no price . . .

I thank thee, O Lord,
That thou hast made me wise in thy faith,
and hast given me knowledge in thy wondrous mysteries,
in thy faithful mercies to [. . .] man,
in thy many compassions to the perverse of heart.

Who is like thee among the gods, O Lord;
and who can match thy fidelity?
Who can be justified before thee in his judgement?
No spirit shall argue with thy reproof,
and none shall stand before thee in thine anger.
But all thy faithful children
shalt thou bring in forgiveness before thee,

[cleans]ing them from their iniquities by thy great goodness,
and by the abundance of thy mercies
thou dost cause them to stand before thee,
for ever and ever.

For an everlasting God art thou,
And all thy ways are established for eternity
and there is none beside thee . . .

During the night, as some slept in their tents and huts under the cliffs round about, and their brethren in the Settlement kept up this continual chant of hymns and readings, some of the elders would be standing in the watch-tower, gazing at the skies, noting the movements of the moon and stars. We have a number of their works referring to the movements of the heavenly bodies, and not all their study was of purely academic interest. For them the stars and their positions could affect men's lives, and amongst their esoteric documents we have one describing the influence of the heavenly bodies on the physical and spiritual characteristics of those born in certain sections of the Zodiac. One man will be hairy, or long-limbed, or stumpy-fingered, or, more important, be possessed of an abundance or otherwise of the Good Spirit, so that his whole being will be affected according to the sign of the Zodiac which he may claim for his own. And above all, they doubtless looked for a particular constellation which would tell them of a special birth, the coming of One for whom they and the whole Jewish world waited. We need not look far from Bethlehem to find a school of thought from which the Magi story of Matthew could have come.

Sacrificial Ritual and the Calendar

As already mentioned in Chapter Six, there is some evidence which points to the Sect's having their own sanctuary at Qumran. The 'Mosaic' regulation concerning the centralization of Temple sacrifice (Deuteronomy xii.5), was usually taken, of course, to mean Jerusalem. But as participation in the Temple cult was no longer possible to the Sectarian since the place and its ordinances had suffered defilement, the Community had found another 'place which the Lord your God shall choose'. Originally, as we have seen, it was the officiating of a spurious High Priest which had made the Temple sacrifices of no account, but in the Qumran documents we can also see another major point of difference between the Sect and the Jerusalem priesthood and cult. At Qumran, the Community was observing a different calendar from that in use in Jerusalem. Thus, in their eyes, all the Temple ritual there was being observed on the wrong days of the year and its efficacy thus hopelessly impaired. Something of the Calendar controversy reaches us from pseudepigraphal literature which, as we shall see, is closely connected with, if not emanating from, our Sect. Thus in the Books of the Heavenly Luminaries in Enoch, we have instructions vouchsafed by Enoch to Methusaleh, his son, as revealed to him by the angel Uriel. For the author, the year is composed of twelve months of thirty days each, with one day intercalated for each of the seasons, making 364 in all, and exactly fifty-two weeks. Thus the festivals will recur on exactly the same day each week of the year, as ordained 'in the heavenly tablets'. This again is the main preoccupation of the book of Jubilees, a work which purports to give the chronology of the principal events in Israel's history to the very day of the week. This work was a great favourite of the Sect, as we know from the five fragmentary copies recovered from the Fourth Cave, and it is quoted in the *Damascus Document*, which says:

> And the statement of the epochs of Israel's blindness to all these may be learnt in the Book of the Divisions of the Times into their jubilees and weeks.

And Enoch similarly points to the defection of men in not recognizing this ideal division of the periods:

> in this men have gone astray, and are accordingly not to be numbered among the righteous.

The difficulty with this ideal calendar, of course, is that it does not fit the natural phenomena. As every schoolboy knows, the year consists of 365 and a quarter days, not of 364, and over a long period of years the difference is quite considerable. It seems probable that the error was rectified by the intercalation of a 'jubilee year,' not a full calendar year but an interval after the end of each 'jubilee' of forty-nine years so that the Calendar could catch up on the solar cycle. The *Manual* has a section on the seasons which speaks of

> the seasons of the years to their weeks (of years), at the beginning of their weeks to a season of liberation,

the last phrase presumably meaning this jubilee period of intercalation. Furthermore, scholars have recently shown that this old Jubilees calendar has a history going right back to the Exile, being used probably by Ezekiel, the priestly redactor of the Pentateuch, and the Chronicler to whom we owe the books of Chronicles and Ezra–Nehemiah.

One of the most hated innovations of the Hellenistic movement was the introduction of the Greek lunar calendar, with the periodic insertion of an intercalary month. Naturally, as with the language, day-to-day intercourse would make some sort of standardization of the calendar absolutely essential, but the Sect and other conservative bodies of Judaism saw this as just one more step in the abandonment of the faith of their forefathers and fiercely resisted it. One is reminded of the protests made in certain quarters in our own country at the introduction of daylight saving. But this went deeper for people like our Covenanters, for, particularly since the Exile, a great deal of the personal religious faith of the Jew centred in the Temple cult and observance of the festivals. It was thus a matter of vital importance for his whole religious life that those rites should be performed on the correct, and thus most efficacious, days. To break tradition on this point was to nullify the whole Temple ritual.

We know, however, of one rite peculiar to Qumran which probably became the sacramental focus of their worship, just as basically the same act did for the Christian Church.

This was the Messianic Banquet, which is described for us in some detail in the *Manual*:

> [This is (the order of) the ses]sion of men of repute, [who are called] to meet for the Council of the Community. When [God] begets the Messiah with them, there shall come [the Priest], head of all the Congregation of Israel, and all the priests, e[lders of the children of] Aaron, [invited] to the Meeting as men of repute. And they shall sit be[fore him, each] according to his rank, corresponding to his st[ation] in the camps and marches. And all the heads of the el[ders of the Congregation] shall sit before them, each man according to his rank. And [when] they are gathered at the communion ta[ble, or to drink] the new wi[ne], and the communion table is laid out, and the new wine [mixed] for drinking, [let no man stretch forth] his hand on the first of the bread or the [wine] before the Priest; for [he will bl]ess the first of the bread and win[e, and will stretch forth] his hand on the bread first.
>
> And after[wards], the Messiah will str[etch forth] his hands upon the bread, [and then] all the Congregation of the Community [will give bles]sings, each [according to] his rank. And after this prescription shall they act for every ass[embly where] at least ten men are assembled.

The chief actors in the Qumran Sect's Messianic Banquet, then, are the two Messiahs, i.e., the High Priest and the lay or Davidic Messiah, of whom we shall speak later, the priests, the heads of the thousands of Israel, the elders and the Congregation. This will be the pattern of the Banquet to be held for the Elect who survive the great purging of the world in the last days. The last sentence, however, makes it clear that it could be a frequently observed ceremony involving far fewer participants than the numbers of the true Israel in the apocalyptic ideal, and since elsewhere in the *Manual* we have reference to the customary blessing of the bread and wine before partaking of the daily meal, it seems probable that every communal repast was considered to some extent a rehearsal of the Messianic Banquet. On the other hand, there is some evidence for a periodic observance of this act which exceeds in scope and importance the day-to-day communal feeding. In a trench dug through an open space near the Monastery walls, the archaeologists found some fifty jars or pots containing the bones of joints of meat, which had been boiled or roasted and picked quite clean. The animals involved were sheep, goats, and a calf, and were clearly the remains of meals, and presumably sacred meals, since considerable care and expense had been spent on keeping the bones free from pollution. The cooking bowls, for instance, were in some cases still quite complete and perfectly usable. They obviously could not be the remains of the daily repasts, since the number of burials would have had to run into tens of thousands, and, in any case, it is hardly likely that the Sectarians would be luxuriating every day on meat. They could, however, be the remains of an annual sacred meal, and one thinks at once of the Passover, which is not without its messianic connexions in later Judaism. However, it must be admitted that so far we have recovered no definite evidence linking the Messianic Banquet with the Passover.

Another curious fact for the life of the Sect emerges from a study of the Jubilees calendar. One of the strict injunctions of that work is that the Feast of Weeks must fall in the middle of the third month, i.e. the fifteenth day. This raises a problem at once, since the Law demands that this Feast must occur fifty days after the offering of the first sheaf, which was 'on the morrow of the Sabbath' (Lev. xxiii. 15–16). In the Jubilees calendar of a thirty-day month, this means that the point of departure must be the twenty-sixth of the first month, Nisan. But a Sabbath on the twenty-fifth of the month is impossible to a Jubilees calendar if the first day of creation and thus of the first week of the year was a Sunday. Sundays would then be on the first, eighth, fifteenth, twenty-second, and twenty-ninth days of the first month. The only way the Jubilees injunction could be made to work in practice would be if the year began on a

Wednesday, giving Saturdays on the fourth, eleventh, eighteenth, and twenty-fifth days of the first month. Now from Exodus xii. 6 we learn that the Passover began on the fifteenth day of the first month, which under this system would be a Wednesday, and in a 364-day year would always be on the same day. The offering of the sheaf, then, on the twenty-sixth day would occur on the morrow of the Sabbath which follows the week of unleavened bread of the Passover festival. Mademoiselle Jaubert has made a particular study of the subject, and her examination of the patriarchs' movements recorded in Jubilees shows that the day most carefully avoided in their time-table, and thus the Sabbath, was not the *seventh* day of the week but the *fourth,* showing clearly that the Jubilees calendar began the year on the fourth day of the week, Wednesday, on the principle that it was only on that day that the heavenly luminaries were created, and thus one could not properly speak of 'day and night' before that (Genesis i. 14–19).

This reverence for Wednesday as the first day of the week has some rather interesting parallels which may not be unconnected with our Sect. A Jew of the first half of the tenth century, by name Al Qirqisānī, mentions in his book a certain religious sect called the *Maghārīya,* or Cave Sect, because their books were found in a cave (*maghār*), and places them historically after the Pharisees and before the Christians, but does not give their ancient name. These same people also receive mention by two Muslim authors, Al Bīrūnī (d. 1048) and Shahrastānī (d. 1153) both of whom seem to have been dependent on a lost ninth-century work on the *History of Religions.* Al Bīrūnī says of the calendar of the Cave Sect that it was on the night between the third and the fourth days, i.e. Tuesday night, that they

> counted the days and months, and the great cycle of feasts commenced then, for it was on the fourth day that God created the great luminaries. Similarly according to them, Passover commenced on Wednesday.

Al Qirqisānī was of the Jewish sect called the Karaites, and it is remarkable that Karaite writings of the ninth and tenth centuries begin to show many points of correspondence with the Qumran Sect, which we shall discuss when looking at similar correspondences elsewhere about this time. But in connexion with the calendar, it is interesting to note that the thirteenth-century chronicle of Bar Hebraeus mentions certain disputes which arose in the ninth century at Tiberias, where the Karaites were being accused of profaning the Sabbath and solemnizing *Wednesday*.

CHAPTER EIGHT

OTHER WORKS FROM THE QUMRAN LIBRARY

THE Sect possessed many books which were not finally included in the biblical Canon, and which appear in the Protestant Apocrypha or have been collected under the title of *Pseudepigrapha.* Thus fragments of the original Hebrew version of the book of Ecclesiasticus, or the Wisdom of Ben Sira, were found in one of the Qumran caves. Tobit also has appeared, one copy in Hebrew and the other in Aramaic. Previously known mainly in the Greek recension, this is the first time we have seen the book in its oldest Semitic form.

We have already noted that the book of Jubilees was a great favourite with the Sect, and it has appeared in five different manuscripts, one of them being written on papyrus. Previously the only certainly known versions of this work were in Ethiopic and Latin, and it is exciting to see the book in its original tongue and to compare these translations which seem, on the whole, to have been quite faithful to their original. The book of Enoch was another staunch favourite of the Community, and has appeared in eight different manuscripts, all in Aramaic, but possessing a very complex relationship to the Greek and Ethiopic versions so far known. Some sections seem to be entirely missing from these versions, such as a letter from Enoch to Shamazya and his companions which appears in the Qumran collection. Other parts are missing from Qumran although represented in the later translations, whilst several sections, particularly the astronomical part III, seem to have had a separate circulation, though not always in the precise form of the later translations.

One of the most important works of the *Pseudepigrapha* is that called *The Testaments of the Twelve Patriarchs,* which purports to give the last words of the twelve Israelite patriarchs to their sons.

Some parts of this work have long been recognized as Christian in origin, although the nucleus of the work was as clearly Jewish. Just how far Christian interpolation extends through the complete work has been a matter of great contention amongst scholars, and naturally it was of supreme importance to have pre-Christian copies of any part of this work to estimate the probable original strata. Now from the Qumran library we are able to see fragments of copies of the Testament of Levi in their original Aramaic, and incidentally, containing a portion of Chapter Fourteen which has generally been supposed to have been one of the later interpolated sections.

The very important *Manual of Discipline,* found nearly complete in the First Cave, has appeared in eleven different manuscripts represented by the fragments, and very significantly for the history of the Sect and their ideas, these versions show some differences which can be traced to the process of compilation and selection. The oldest of these manuscripts goes back probably to the very beginning of the Sect, so that the work has clearly had a long and involved history.

The *Damascus Document* has appeared in seven different manuscripts, one of which is on papyrus, and some of the fragments have sections missing from the medieval copies from which we have hitherto known the work (see Appendix II). Thus, for example, parts of the original beginning and end are now extant, and we have part of the final summing up of the work in the words:

> and this is the explanation of the ordinances which they shall carry out throughout the whole of the period of [. . .] concerning the interpretation of the Last Torah.

This last phrase is particularly important for understanding the attitude of the Sect towards their own sectarian documents, which carried over, as it were, the Mosaic Law until the time of the coming of the One who could make a final interpretation, the Last Law of all for the new age.

A very important group of manuscripts again for the understanding of the calendar of the Sect are those containing the various roles of the priestly families, their weeks, feasts, and years of service, and a papyrus document constitutes a collection of evening and morning prayers for every day of the month.

A well-represented group of pseudo-prophetical literature has appeared, much of it previously quite unknown. Included in this are the remains of five or six copies of a composition which is clearly modelled on the style of our book of Jeremiah, rather like the apocryphal Jeremiah–Baruch literature already known, yet not textually identical with any portion of it.

From the First Cave came an almost complete work giving the order of battle for an apocalyptic war between what are called 'the Sons of Light' and 'the Sons of Darkness' and four fragmentary copies have been found in the Fourth Cave which help fill out some of the lacunae in the large scroll. The combatants are further detailed as the Jews of Levitic, Judahite, and Benjamite ancestry, and their opponents are the forces of Edom, Moab, Ammon, and Philistia on the one hand, and the 'Kittim' on the other. The army of the Children of Light is based on a general mobilization of the people between the ages of fifteen and thirty, the cavalry corps between thirty and forty-five, officers between forty and fifty, commanders between fifty and sixty. The formal and artificial nature of these 'Queen's Regulations' will be apparent from the first, and continues in laying down a sevenfold volley from the slingers which precedes seven throws from the javelin throwers, who in turn open the way for the attack of the phalanx. All the operations are directed by the priests, who sound off the trumpet calls, 'Advance', 'Attack', 'Retreat', 'Reassembly', 'Pursuit', and 'Ambush'. Before the attack, the whole army gives a great shout to strike terror in the heart of the enemy.

The Head Priest accompanies the army into the field, and prayers precede and follow the battle. Further indications that this is a religious war are contained in the mottoes of the banners which precede the various sections into battle. Thus before the main body goes the slogan 'People of God' with the names of Israel and Aaron and the twelve tribes of Israel. Before the regiments goes the strange device,

> The Wrath of God will burn against Belial and against the Men whose Lot is with him until None Survives.

Company standards had,

> From God comes the force of battle against all Wicked Flesh,

and platoons were preceded by

> The place of the Power of Evil Men shall cease through the might of God.

Each squad carried

> Joyful praises with the harp (be unto) God.

Besides these there were special banners for the various stages of the conflict, all of which were laid down, including the temporary reversal. Thus on entering the field,

> Truth of God, Righteousness of God, Glory of God, Judgement of God,

was displayed above all. When the army closed with the enemy they were cheered and the foes overcome with

> The Right Hand of God, the Appointed Time of God, the Tumult of God, the Slain of God.

On retirement, the Children of Light carried with them

> The Adoration of God, the Greatness of God, the Praises of God, the Glory of God.

Even the trumpets had mottoes. For instance the ones used for signalling pursuit had on them the apposite message:

> God smiteth all the Children of Darkness; let not His Anger subside until they are destroyed.

After an initial defeat, the apocalyptic victory is won, and the victorious army returns to camp, and

> Joyfully sing the hymn of returning, and the next morning wash their clothes and cleanse themselves of the blood of the guilty corpses, and return to the site of their stand where they had drawn up their army before the dead of the enemy fell.

There they all bless God together, saying,

> Blessed be the God of Israel who is faithful to His Covenant and the testimonies of salvation for the people redeemed by Him.

Mr Yadin, the head of a more recent Jewish army, who has edited this work for the Hebrew University, claims to be able to find in its basic strategy correspondences with the Roman army manuals of the day, whilst others have thought that, although it reflects a genuine method of warfare, it might be more akin to the Maccabean practices. But the apocalyptic nature of the battle it describes is clear, and when one stands in the middle of the pathetic ruins of their humble Settlement buildings at Qumran, and powders the charred remains of their roofs between the fingers, the dream of their Final War against the powers of Darkness and the reality of their conflict with a more material enemy seem worlds apart.

CHAPTER NINE

THE DOCTRINES OF THE SECT

THE basic philosophical and religious conception of the Sect is contained in their doctrine of the Two Spirits. Briefly this implies that there are in the Universe two spirits, one of good and the other of evil, respectively symbolized as Light and Darkness. Both are under the same supreme rule of God who will eventually give the victory to Good, but only after a prolonged cosmic battle. The war of the Spirits is reflected on earth in the tensions within every man for good and evil, as the *Manual* says:

> And He assigned to Man two Spirits in which he should walk until the time of His visitation. They are the spirits of Truth and Perversity: Truth born out of the spring of Light, Perversity from the well of Darkness. The dominion of all the children of righteousness is in the hands of the Prince of Lights so that they walk in the ways of Light, whereas the government of the children of Perversity is in the hands of the Angel of Darkness, to walk in the ways of Darkness. The purpose of the Angel of Darkness is to lead all the children of righteousness astray, and all their sin, their iniquities, their guilt and their rebellious works are the result of his domination, in accordance with God's mysteries until His appointed time. And all their stripes and seasons of affliction are consequent upon the rule of his (Satan's) hostility.

Thus the whole cosmos is divided for the time being into two camps, and as Man is apportioned these two spirits so will he behave:

> Until now the Spirits of Truth and Perversity struggle within the heart of Man, behaving with wisdom and folly. And according as a man inherits truth and righteousness, so will he hate Perversion, but in so far as his

> heritage is rather from the side of perversion and wickedness, so shall he loathe the Truth.

Another document tells us that his 'inheriting' of these Spirits depends on the stars at his birth, and even that the proportions within a man can be numerically reckoned.

Here are the fruits of the Spirit of Truth as enumerated in the *Manual*:

> To enlighten the heart of Man and to make straight before him all the ways of true righteousness, to make his heart fearful for the judgements of God; a humble spirit, an even temper, a freely compassionate nature, an eternal goodness, and understanding and insight and mighty wisdom which believes in all God's works, and a confident trust in His many mercies, and a spirit of knowledge in every ordered work, and zeal for righteous judgements, and a determined holiness with steadfast mind; loyal feelings towards all the children of Truth, and a radiant purity which loathes every impure idol; a humble bearing and a discretion regarding all the hidden things of Truth and secrets of Knowledge.

The reward to those who show these qualities in their lives is

> healing and abundant peace, length of life and fruitful seed with everlasting blessings, and eternal joy in immortality, a crown of glory and a robe of majesty in eternal light.

To be contrasted with this sublime state is the lot of those led by the Spirit of Perversion. Among the fruits of their Spirit is greed, injustice, wickedness, falsehood, pride, deceit, hasty temper, jealousy, lechery, blasphemy, spiritual obtuseness, and obstinacy, and vile cunning. No wonder that the best he can expect in the 'Day of Visitation' is

> many stripes from the Angels of Destruction, in the everlasting Pit, through the overwhelming God of Vengeance, in everlasting terror and perpetual disgrace, with the shame of extermination in the Fire of the dark regions. And all their times for all generations will be in grievous mourning and bitter misfortune, in the dark calamities until they are destroyed with no chance to escape.

Since the Spirits are apportioned at birth, this apparent determinism may seem to override the bounds of justice. If a man, by his stars, is given a balance of evil in his character it seems hardly fair to condemn him to such punishment for eternity. The argument will have a familiar ring in these days of popular psychology, but the Qumran Covenanter, at least, had his answer. For all men there was one way of salvation, depending on his own will and the mercy of God. If he would but apply himself to the study of God's Word in humility and pious devotion, God would answer by granting him a restored cleanliness, a sense of perfection.

> For it is . . . through the submission of his soul to the statutes of God that his flesh may be cleansed ('flesh' being here exactly the Pauline *sarx,* the debased moral nature of Man) . . . He will order his steps in the perfect Way and in all the paths of God . . . not transgressing a single one of His words.

Man must prepare himself by self-discipline, but the action of cleansing is entirely dependent on the will of God. Man has no claim to justification merely on the grounds of his good works; it is an act of divine grace, as much in the eyes of the Covenanter as of Paul.

> As for me [says the psalmist at the end of the *Manual*], my justification belongs to God, and in His hand is the perfection of my way . . . and from the fountain of His righteousness (springs) my justification, a light in my heart.

And again,

> if I totter, the covenant love of God is my eternal salvation, and if I stumble in the crookedness of my flesh, my justification depends on the righteousness of God, which is eternal.

The word used here for 'justification' is *mishpaṭ,* which also means 'judgement'. Man's justification is the pronounced verdict of God, a legal 'clearing' which by no means implies sinlessness. Rather, Man's iniquity has been cleansed by the grace of God: he is restored into true sonship and, in the words of another passage of the *Manual*, 'estimated perfect'.

In all this, many of my Christian readers will have begun to feel the warmth of a familiar hearth. Here are the ideas of the New Covenant, the emphasis on justification by grace and a doctrine of perfection. We are indeed bordering very closely on to Christian soil and must accordingly begin to weave our threads of Qumran theology into the fabric of the New Testament to understand fully the considerable significance of the new material for the history of the Church.

Let us first return to the basic doctrine of the Two Spirits. The richest source of New Testament comparison is certainly in the writings of St John. In his first Epistle there is hardly a paragraph which does not contain some reference to the opposition of Light and Darkness, of Truth and Error (a legitimate translation of '*āwôn*, 'perversion', at root, anything 'twisted').

> God is Light, and in Him is no darkness at all. If we say that we have fellowship with Him, and walk in darkness, we lie, and do not the truth (a favourite Qumran phrase): but if we walk in the Light, as He is in the Light, we have fellowship one with another (i. 5–7).

The spirits of this world must be tested and proved according to their response to the central fact of creation, the Messiahship of Jesus:

> Beloved, believe not every spirit, but prove the spirits, whether they are of God: because many false prophets are gone out into the world . . . Hereby know ye the Spirit of God: every spirit which confesseth that Jesus Christ is come in the flesh is of God: and every spirit which confesseth not Jesus is not of God (iv. 1–3).

Perhaps most familiar is the Prologue of the Gospel:

> In him was life; and the life was the Light of men. And the Light shineth in the darkness; and the darkness apprehendeth it not . . . There was the true Light, *even the Light* which lighteth every man coming into the world (i. 4–5, 9).

It is a fact that the Qumran library has profoundly affected the study of the Johannine writings and many long-held conceptions have had to be radically revised. No longer can John be regarded as the most Hellenistic of the Evangelists; his 'gnosticism' and the whole framework of his thought is seen now to spring directly from a Jewish sectarianism rooted in Palestinian soil, and his material recognized as founded in the earliest layers of Gospel traditions.

In 'the Light which lighteth every man' we have explicitly the idea of apportionment of the Spirit of Light to Man at birth, and perhaps the enigmatic phrase in iii. 34,

> for he giveth not the Spirit by measure

has reference to the numerical division of Qumran. To John, the apportionment of the Spirit of Light to Jesus was such that he became Light itself: 'I am the Light of the world', and he records that the promise to those about him who would believe on him and his mission was that they should become 'sons of Light', the exact terminology used by the Sect to describe themselves in the apocalyptic war with the 'sons of Darkness'. Jesus speaks of a 'second birth' when a Man would 'be born of the water and the Spirit', and we might recall the Qumran psalm which speaks of God purifying

> some of the sons of man to abolish the spirit of perversion from his flesh, and to cleanse him by His Holy Spirit from all wicked deeds, and sprinkle on him the Spirit of Truth as purifying water.

Just as the Qumran sectarians waited for the final vindication of the Spirit of Light at the Time of Visitation, so to John, in a different perspective,

> the darkness is passing away, and the true Light already shineth (I. ii. 8).

This opposition of Light and Darkness, Truth and error, comes clearly enough from Iranian thought, but it did not develop into an absolute dualism at Qumran as it did there. Both good and bad spirits are subject to God, although, naturally enough here, as in John, we are coming perilously near to a dualism in the personification of the Spirit of Evil in the Angel of Darkness, or Belial for Qumran, and Satan, the Devil, the 'Prince of this world', 'murderer from the beginning', for John. Demon possession is a necessary corollary of this doctrine, and of course occurs time and time again in the gospel stories, particularly in the healing miracles. Jesus used his authority as one abundantly 'possessed' of the opposite Spirit, to cast out the powers of darkness in the mentally sick. Thus his enemies' assertion that he was the Devil himself was quite absurd:

> and if Satan casteth out Satan, he is divided against himself . . . But if I by the Spirit of God cast out devils, then is the kingdom of God come upon you (Matt. xii. 26–8).

If Jesus is demonstrating the power of the Spirit of Light in this way against the powers of Darkness, it can only mean that the cosmic battle is nearing its climax in the universe, and the 'rule' or 'kingdom' of God is being wonderfully demonstrated in the world. God has at last come to the aid of a divided mankind, in the person of His Messiah, or Prince of Light, who enters the house of Satan, 'the strong man' and despoils it. The moral issues of the world take on their true colours: no longer do the greys and half-whites plague man's decisions, but he is confronted with blacks and whites, and the choice is clear-cut:

> He that is not with me is against me (Matt. xii. 30).

To be kept constantly in mind when reading Qumran literature, as also the New Testament, is the sense of impending doom which pervaded religious thought of this time, and which at intervals, has done so ever since. We have already seen that the Qumran sectarians went into the desert to prepare for the Day of Visitation, and from there they viewed the terrible events in their land and read them as the 'signs of the times'. Jesus, too, is aware of a special tension in the world, coming to a climax as he faced his death, in which the Spirits of Darkness would make their final bid for supremacy, but which would, in its victory, usher in the new age. This time of trial would be shared by all living in those days, for in every man the forces of evil would increase their struggle against the powers of Light and Truth as the end drew near. It was a time of Temptation (*peirasmos* of the New Testament), and Jesus' hope for his followers was that they should be spared this terrible conflict within their hearts which he himself was undergoing as representative of mankind.

'Pray that ye enter not into temptation' is the keynote of his last messages, and when the climax was drawing near, and the forces of Darkness drew themselves together for the supreme battle, he bade his disciples keep awake in the Garden: 'Watch and pray, that ye enter not into temptation.' His pattern of prayer again sounds this note of urgency, though over-repetition would seem to have blunted it for most of us. 'Thy kingdom come' is no vague hope for the morrow, but a cry of anguish from the bottom of a tortured soul for the end of the Age, a release from the spiritual battle which the new age of Light and goodness would bring.

'Lead us not into temptation but deliver us from evil' is the plea of a soul battling within itself as the powers of darkness begin to pit their strength against an awakened conscience.

The Mysteries

> Now God, through the mysteries of His understanding and His glorious wisdom, has ordained a set period for Perversion, and in the time of His visitation He will destroy it for ever. Then shall the Truth of the universe shine forth for all time.

Thus speaks the *Manual of Discipline;* now listen to Paul in his letter to the Romans:

> according to the revelation of the mystery which hath been kept in silence through times eternal, but now is manifested (xvi. 25–26).

And again to the Corinthians:

> but we speak God's wisdom in a mystery, *even* the *wisdom* that hath been hidden, which God foreordained before the worlds unto our glory: which none of the rulers of this world knoweth: for had they known it, they would not have crucified the Lord of glory . . . But unto us God revealed *it* through the Spirit: for the Spirit searcheth all things, yea, the deep things of God (I. ii. 7–10).

And speaking to the Ephesians:

> . . . how that by revelation was made known unto me the mystery, as I wrote afore in a few words, whereby, when ye read, ye can perceive my understanding in the mystery of Christ; which in other generations was not made known unto the sons of men, as it hath now been revealed unto his holy apostles and prophets in the Spirit . . . ; unto me . . . was this grace given, to preach unto the Gentiles the unsearchable riches of Christ: and to make all men see what is the dispensation of the mystery which from all ages hath been hid in God who created all things (iii. 3–9).

So possession of the Holy Spirit was to Paul a means of unlocking these divine 'mysteries'. The Teacher of Righteousness of the Qumran Community also had access to these secrets, as we learn from the commentary on Habakkuk:

> to whom God made known all the secrets of the words of His servants, the prophets.

The 'mystery' theme, originally traceable to Persian thought and found to some extent even in orthodox Judaism, is very common in Qumran literature, and again there can be little doubt that Paul was standing in a direct line of tradition with our Sectarians when he used the idea and, indeed, at times the exact terminology of the Scrolls in this connexion. But, as in his doctrine of justification and redemption, Paul is looking primarily to the work and person of Jesus as the source of grace and knowledge of the mysteries. For Paul, this process of revelation, making the unknown God 'knowable', was now available not only to

'God's servants the prophets' but even to the Gentiles through the universality of the Messiah.

Knowledge

Penetration of the mysteries gives access to a supernatural knowledge. This was not so much the result of intellectual exercise, as a heavenly revelation, the nature of which in the Dead Sea Scrolls, as in Christianity, is almost entirely eschatological. Thus Matthew records that when Jesus was speaking about the Day of Judgement, he went on,

> I thank thee, O Father, Lord of Heaven and Earth, that Thou didst hide these things from the wise and understanding, and didst reveal them unto babes . . . All these things have been delivered unto me of my Father: and no one knoweth the Son save the Father; neither doth any know the Father save the Son, and he to whomsoever the Son willeth to reveal *Him* (xi. 25–27).

The *Manual of Discipline* says:

> He will purge by His truth all the deeds of Men . . . to give to the upright insight into the knowledge of the Most High and into the wisdom of the sons of Heaven, to give the perfect of way understanding.

'The Sons of Heaven' are the angels who sit in the divine council chamber, and who thus have pre-knowledge of the celestial plans of operation, from which will ultimately result the apocalyptic acts or 'works of God'. Thus the Spirit of Truth enlightens a man to

> an understanding and insight and mighty wisdom which believes in all the works of God.

The same phrase exactly is used in the Gospels; thus John records:

> They said therefore unto him, What must we do, that we may work the works of God? Jesus answered . . . This is the work of God, that ye believe on him whom He hath sent. They said therefore unto him, What then doest thou for a sign, that we may see, and believe thee? (vi. 28–30).

But the sign that Jesus gave, of healing the sick and casting out devils, they misunderstood, and on being questioned he replied,

> Neither did this man sin, nor his parents: but that the works of God should be made manifest in him (ix. 3).

We have already seen examples of this type of eschatalogical knowledge in the Bible commentaries of the Sect. The interpreters are here delving into the words of Scripture in order to lay bare by allegorical method the divine secrets of the last times, and, in much the same way, the early Church went to their Bibles to seek there references to the Messiah Jesus. Matthew, especially, abounds in such 'throw-backs' into the Old Testament to explain events in Jesus' life and aspects of his work. Some of them are as artificial, and to us as unconvincing, as any of the expositions of the Qumran commentaries, but we must remember that for the early Jewish-Christian Church an 'objective' life of Jesus would have been as pointless as one of the Teacher for the Qumran Community: to attempt to read 'connected history' into the expositions of the Qumran commentators is completely to misunderstand their purpose.

It is worth our while to turn aside for the moment to look more closely into this question of the Qumran and New Testament use of Scripture as a pointer to the solution of a number of problems connected with both.

CHAPTER TEN

THE USE OF SCRIPTURE TEXTS IN THE DEAD SEA SCROLLS AND THE NEW TESTAMENT

VERY briefly, the problem of New Testament citations of scripture is this: certain writers, and particularly Matthew, cite Old Testament passages in a way at variance with every textual tradition which has come down to us. That they should often follow the LXX against the Hebrew is to be expected, since the LXX was the Bible of the early Church, and it is also understandable that some of the quotations should have been taken from the Hebrew Scriptures, especially among the Jewish-Christian writers. What is more puzzling is where they quote a version which is otherwise completely unknown. Here are some examples.

In Matthew ii. 6, the evangelist is showing how Christ's birth was foretold by the prophets of old as taking place in Bethlehem, and to prove his point he quotes:

> And thou, Bethlehem, land of Judah, art in no wise least among the princes of Judah: for out of thee shall come forth a governor, which shall be a shepherd of my people Israel.

Now Micah v. 2 actually says:

> But thou, Bethlehem Ephrathah, which art little to be among the families of Judah, out of thee shall one come forth unto me that is to be ruler in Israel.

LXX differs little and no support for Matthew can be found in the other versions. But he has changed the whole sentence structure, implying that Bethlehem is not the least, whereas the Hebrew says he is, adds the conjunction 'for' to give his rendering any sense, alters 'families' (or 'thousands') to 'princes', omits 'unto me' and elaborates 'Israel' with 'my people'. The modernizing of the geography, 'Ephrathah' to 'land of Judah' is the least of his variants.

We have seen something of how the idea of the 'mysteries' and divine 'knowledge' permeates New Testament writings. Matthew finds some support for this idea in explaining Jesus' use of parables by quoting Psalm lxxviii. 2 in the form:

> I will open my mouth in parables; I will utter things hidden from the foundation of the world (xiii. 35).

This is how the Psalmist's Hebrew is usually rendered:

> I will open my mouth in a parable; I will utter dark sayings of old; which we have heard and known, and our fathers have told us.

Again Matthew has no support from the versions.

Palm Sunday's events are justified by Matthew by a particularly interesting composite quotation:

> Tell ye the daughter of Zion, Behold, thy King cometh unto thee, meek, and riding upon an ass, and upon a colt the foal of an ass (xxi. 5).

This is how the Hebrew of Zechariah ix. 9 may be read:

> Rejoice greatly, O daughter of Zion; shout O daughter of Jerusalem: Behold thy King cometh unto thee; he is just, and having salvation; lowly and riding upon an ass, even upon a colt the foal of an ass.

In Isaiah lxii. 11 we find:

> Say ye to the daughter of Zion, Behold thy salvation cometh.

Clearly both quotations have been joined together, but its composite nature is not the only peculiarity of this use of Scripture by Matthew. In his rendering he has divided the parallel stichoi of the Hebrew verse to imply that there were two separate animals involved, an ass and a colt. Note that the English version renders the Hebrew

> an ass, even upon a colt . . .

to show, quite rightly, that the one is in the Hebrew merely a synonym of the other. Mark and Luke speak of only one animal, but Matthew's quotation leads him in verse 7 into the apparent absurdity of the disciples putting their garments on both animals. Certainly the Matthaean school cannot be accused of not knowing Hebrew properly, and it is probable that another tradition is showing through here, possibly pre-Christian in origin.

Now in these three examples quoted, and there are many such, one point is common to all, that Matthew's versions of the texts favour his interpretation of the events. Thus the 'ruler' of Micah ('governor' in Matthew) has been supplemented by the title of 'shepherd', a conception of the Davidic ideal ruler which we see already in II Samuel v. 2 and Ezekiel xxxiv. 23 from which both this and the addition, 'my people', have come. The loose 'families' has been crystallized into 'princes', and 'Bethlehem' is made 'not least' among his compatriots, and geographically clarified. All of which fits into the pattern of Jesus, the Davidic Messiah, who was born in Bethlehem, at least according to this early tradition; but it can hardly be considered an 'objective' reading of Scripture. Similarly, the divergencies of the second example need not be referred back to a variant Hebrew tradition. It is clear that the Old Testament text concerned containing

> which we have heard and known, and our fathers have told us

hardly fits in with the doctrine of revealed eschatological Knowledge we have just been discussing, and the singular 'parable' has been made plural to apply to Jesus' words. In the last example, Matthew has read his Hebrew quite illegitimately from a literary point of view possibly in order to make it conform to a current tradition involving two animals.

Now it has long been recognized that such paraphrasing has been practised by the New Testament writers, and there are some parallel usages to be found in rabbinic literature, but in the Dead Sea Scrolls we find the same practice and method used time and time again, and there is no hermeneutic principle of interpretation in the New Testament which cannot be exactly matched in the Qumran literature. There are some very good examples in the Habakkuk Commentary of the writer deliberately altering his text to fit his interpretation. In Habakkuk i. 13 the prophet is speaking to the Lord, and says:

> Thou that art of purer eyes than to behold evil and that canst not look upon perverseness.

The commentator interprets this to mean, quite reasonably, that God will not let His people perish in the hands of the Gentiles; rather the Gentiles will fall into the hands of the Elect. But in the next part of the verse,

> wherefore lookest Thou upon them that deal treacherously, and holdest Thy peace when the wicked swalloweth up the man that is more righteous than he,

whilst the prophet is still, of course, addressing God, the commentator fastens immediately upon the persecution of the Teacher by the Wicked Priest theme and makes it ask a renegade element of the Sect, called the 'House of Absalom', why they stood by when the righteous Priest suffered. But to do this, he must change the singular 'lookest Thou' to the plural 'look ye', and does so in his quotation, although, needless to say, a plural in the text read consecutively makes nonsense.

Again in ii. 5, where the prophet is making a personification of wine, 'the treacherous dealer', who

> enlargeth his desire as Hell . . . and cannot be satisfied,

the commentator writes in his text *hwn*, 'wealth' for Habakkuk's *hyyn* 'the wine', a very slight orthographic change certainly but giving a very different meaning and according very well with what he wanted to say about the greed of the Wicked Priest in contrast to the avowed poverty of the Sect.

Sometimes, the commentator will change the text of his quotation and then use not only the new version but the old as well, and derive his interpretation from both! Thus in ii. 15, a condemnation of the deliberate intoxication of one's neighbour 'that thou mayest look upon his nakedness', the word for 'nakedness' has been given a very slight orthographic change and read 'their seasons'. This does not give a particular meaningful sense in the context, but it does mean that the commentator can play on the 'nakedness' of the original and introduces a root meaning 'strip' which is closely similar to another meaning 'exile', from which he draws the picture of the Teacher being pursued and persecuted in exile, and uses his 'seasons' to bring in the fact that the persecution took place in the 'season' of rest, the Day of Atonement.

In other places this astute author finds the words to suit his commentary not by changing the text but by using a traditional variant of which he seemed to know, and which we sometimes have preserved for us in some Targum or Midrashic work, and will sometimes proceed to use both traditions in his commentary. He may even split a word and use its two parts, or, leaving the orthography of the text as it stands, use more than one meaning for one of the words involved and comment on both.

Even the New Testament 'compound' quotation is to be found in Qumran. In a group of messianic testimonies, for instance, we find the passage Deuteronomy v. 28–9 run straight on with the famous prophecy of Deuteronomy xviii. 18 in such a way as to give an entirely new meaning to the first text. Thus the Lord says:

> I have heard the voice of the words of this people, which they have spoken unto thee: they have well said all that they have spoken. O that there were such an heart in them, that they would fear me, and keep my commandments always, that it might be well with them, and with their children for ever!

The people, it may be remembered, had been asking for a mediator between themselves and God, and in the verses that follow God appoints Moses to that office. But the purpose of these testimonies is to bring together evidence for the coming of the supreme mediator, the Messiah himself, and the compiler has no compunction in following directly on with the quotation:

> I will raise them up a prophet from among their brethren, like unto thee; and I will put my words in his mouth, and he shall speak unto them all that I shall command him.

Thus the first text no longer refers to Moses, but its theme of mediation is made to apply to the second quotation which, incidentally, is the one used in the New Testament with reference to Jesus, as in the speeches of Peter and Stephen (Acts iii. 22, vii. 37).

This *testimonia* document from Qumran is one of the most important of the works found, and throws new light on one of the most discussed problems of the early Church. It has been argued since the end of the last century that there existed in the Church from the very beginning collections of Old Testament quotations which were used by the fathers in debate and teaching. This theory has some backing from similar collections in use by the Church of later times, which may well, so it has been argued, be based on much earlier documents. Furthermore such a theory would account for the composite quotations found in the New Testament, the ascription of passages to the wrong biblical writers where a number of *testimonia* from various places had been placed together under the name of one prophet, and for the textual variants which seem to persist in certain oft-repeated passages. A recent writer has suggested that the groups of such *testimonia* were gathered together under separate headings such as messianic, legal, apocalyptic, and so on. Although the whole theory has not gone unchallenged, it now seems that we have from Qumran important support for the idea in a pre-Christain collection of eschatalogical *testimonia*, the very first of which is a composite quotation!

Matthew's quotations from the Old Testament fall into two separate groups: those preceded by the formula

> Now this is come to pass, that it might be fulfilled which was spoken by the prophet so-and-so

and the like, and those which are given quite simply without such an introductory phrase or sentence. It has further been observed that whilst the 'formula quotations' tend to follow the Hebrew text of the Bible, the non-formula type agree more with the LXX tradition. It may be no coincidence that this group of unadorned *testimonia* we have been discussing shows marked 'Greek' tendencies, clearly taken from a tradition close to that used by the ancient translators. It seems, therefore, not improbable that certain Jewish sections of the early Church like the Matthew school were using very old groups of *testimonia* in a Hebrew of the pre-Massoretic 'Greek' tradition like so many of our Qumran biblical texts.

Furthermore, it has long been realized that Stephen's speech in the seventh chapter of Acts shows remarkable affinities with the Samaritan recension of the Pentateuch where it quotes the Old Testament. Now that we know that at this very time there were copies of this recension circulating in a strict Jewish community like the Qumran Sect, it seems not improbable that they were also in use by certain sections of the Church.

These correspondences in the use of biblical traditions might now lead us on to consider other similarities between the Church and the Qumran Covenanters.

CHAPTER ELEVEN

THE QUMRAN COMMUNITY AND THE CHURCH

Doctrinal Affinities

FROM a very early stage, the Church seems to have been known as 'those of the Way' or 'the Way of God', which was recognized as a distinct sect (Acts xxiv. 14). This same term is used of the Qumran Covenanters, who, according to the *Manual*, are 'those who choose the Way'. Furthermore, both groups describe themselves as the poor, the children of light, the elect of God, a community of the *New Testament* or *Covenant.* The eighth chapter of the Epistle to the Hebrews quotes in full the Jeremiah passage which is behind this conception, and goes on to describe the Church as a new Temple of God where sacrificial redemption is made once for all for the world. And the Qumran Sect describes itself as

> an eternal planting, a holy house of Israel, a most holy conclave for Aaron, witnesses of Truth in judgement, and chosen by divine favour to atone for the earth, to render to the wicked their deserts. This is the tried wall, the precious corner stone, whose foundation shall not be shaken nor moved from its place.

Extraordinarily similar is Peter's description of the Church:

> ye also, as living stones, are built up a spiritual house to be a holy priesthood, to offer up spiritual sacrifices, acceptable to God through Jesus Christ. Because it is contained in Scripture, Behold, I lay in Zion a chief corner stone, elect, precious . . . But ye are an elect race, a royal priesthood, a holy nation, a people of *God's* own possession . . . (I. ii. 5–9).

Both the Sect and the Christian Church believe they have been given a share in the inheritance of the angels, or holy ones, and both communities see themselves as chosen by God to execute a judgement on the earth at the end of days.

For the Qumran Sect the expiation of the iniquity of the world is achieved by

> practising justice, and the anguish of the refining furnace.

Never far from the conception of this righteous remnant, the True Israel, is the theme of suffering; the oft-referred-to persecution of the Teacher of Righteousness is usually accompanied by the mention of 'his Party', and allusions to the Suffering Servant of Isaiah seem explicit in such phrases as 'witnesses of Truth in judgement' mentioned above, and after the parallel

> Ye are my witnesses, saith the Lord, and my Servant whom I have chosen

in the Servant song of Isaiah 43. In one of their hymns, the Sect pictures itself as a pregnant woman suffering the pangs of parturition as she gives birth to her 'firstborn', the Messiah, who is described in terms reminiscent of the Child of Isaiah ix. 6, the 'Wonderful Counsellor'. Thus the Saviour of the world is to come out of the suffering of the Sect, borne for the atonement of the earth. We shall have to refer again to this obvious parallel with Christian thought when discussing the Messiah of Qumran and the New Testament.

We may perhaps mention here an interesting point which a Qumran text has raised on the subject of Jesus' institution of the Church and Peter's part in it. In a recent publication of an Aramaic fragment of the Testament of Levi from Qumran, Father Milik has drawn attention to and identified a geographical location of particular importance for Jewish apocalypse. It is Abel Mayin, and appears to be situated near one of the sources of the Jordan, overlooked by the towering slopes of Mount Hermon. The special nature of the place which caught the imagination of the Jewish apocalyptists was due to its seeming to communicate both with Heaven on the tops of Hermon and Hell in the deep fount leading into the bowels of the earth from which the Jordan flowed. To this spot were referred a number of important events affecting human and angelic destinies. There the prayer and heavenly vision of Levi took place after he had fallen into a deep sleep (Testament Levi ii. 3–5). Close by, we are told, there was 'a very high mountain, joining heaven to earth' and the Aramaic of the fragment Milik reconstructs to read:

> And I saw the hea[vens opened, and I saw] below me a high [mountain] which reached to the hea[vens, and I remained on it. And] the gates of heaven [were opened] unto me, and an angel [said unto me . . .

Again, Enoch, the Scribe of Righteousness, mediator between God on the one hand and the angels and Man on the other, rejoins the fallen angels assembled at Abel Mayin after seeing visions in a dream and hearing a divine voice speaking to him,

> at the waters of Dan, in the land of Dan, to the south and west of Hermon (xiii. 7).

Milik, in a footnote, draws attention to two New Testament passages which must certainly be reconsidered in the light of this new evidence. The first is that recorded in the sixteenth chapter of Matthew when, in this very area, Peter makes his confession of the messiahship of Jesus, and the Master says,

> thou art Peter, and upon this rock I will build my Church, and the gates of Hades shall not prevail against it. I will give unto thee the keys of the kingdom of Heaven: and whatsoever thou shalt bind on earth shall be bound in heaven; and whatsoever thou shalt loose on earth shall be loosed in heaven (vv. 18–19).

The name *Petros* which Jesus here gives Simon is, in Aramaic, *kēphā'* meaning 'rock'. In the Aramaic fragment referred to, Milik has shown that the missing word for 'mountain' could as easily have been *kēphā'* as the more common *ṭūrā'*, and furthermore, *kēphā'* is the word used in another Qumran Aramaic fragment from the eighty-ninth chapter of the Book of Enoch to describe the 'rock' on which Moses received his revelation for Israel. Historically this was, of course, Sinai, but this mount of revelation near the sources of the Jordan seems to have become a literary figure in Jewish apocalyptic thought to which all the great divine revelations of their history were referred. The story of Peter, the intermediary between God and Man, the 'Rock' with which he is identified in his new name, the 'keys' of heaven and earth implying a mediatorial authority for him as carrying on the tradition of Enoch, Moses, and Levi, the Church as symbolized by this mountain whose top reaches heaven and whose base directly abuts the 'gates of hell', is now clearly seen to stand in this pattern of Jewish apocalypse of the last centuries before Christ.

The other New Testament incident clearly related to this pattern is that of the Transfiguration of Jesus recounted in the following chapter of Matthew and elsewhere. On 'a high mountain apart', long thought to be Hermon, Jesus appeared before Peter and two other disciples in a radiant glory, and is seen speaking with the messianic precursors Moses and Elijah. Again, whatever the historical truth behind this record, the conception of a divine revelation on this particular sacred mountain is seen once more to fit into this well-formed traditional pattern.

Formal Affinities

The Community of Qumran as a whole is given the technical connotation of 'The Many', and is democratically governed by such deliberative councils as we saw described in Chapter Seven. This term appears in its literal translation in the New Testament, and describes the Jerusalem Council of Acts xv. 12 (RV: 'multitude'), the body of the disciples who appointed the Seven (Acts vi. 2, 5), and the congregation of the Antioch Church (Acts xv. 30). It has, furthermore, been suggested that the office of 'Bishop' in the Church has its origin in the Qumran 'Overseer'.

There has long been recognized in the Gospel of Matthew a certain ordering of his material which suggests something in the nature of a handbook for the early Church. It is carefully arranged into five sections, adopts a casuistry in its teaching of moral principles which is almost legal, and has much to say on the position and duties of the Church leaders. A good instance of this method of ordering material on moral discipline is the passage in xviii. 15–17, where the procedure for complaints between the brethren is dealt with and put into the mouth of Jesus. First, reproof is to be made on a personal basis; failing satisfaction it is to be made before one or two witnesses, and if the wrongdoer is still unrepentant, before the whole Church. Only then, if still recalcitrant, may he be banished from the Community. The *Manual* shows the same regulation for the Qumran Sect:

> Let no one speak to his brother in anger, or in grumbling complaint, or with obstinate pride [. . . or] evil spirit; nor shall he hate him [. . .] of his heart, although he may reprove him at that time so as not to incur guilt because of him. Indeed, no man may bring a case against his fellow before the Many which has not first been the subject of a reproof before witnesses.

We saw that the method of priests of the Qumran Community giving their casting vote was by the casting of 'lots'. It will be remembered that this procedure was used in the early Church for finding a replacement for the defaulting Judas:

> And they gave lots for them; and the lot fell upon Matthias; and he was numbered with the eleven disciples (Acts i. 26).

Another correspondence of procedure in both communities is in the pooling of their possessions once they had entered the brotherhood. Deliberate falsification of one's declaration in this respect was a particularly heinous sin in Qumran, as it was in the Church, as we gather from the story of Ananias and Sapphira in Acts 5.

We have earlier described another practice of the Qumran

Community which has its important parallel in the Church, the Messianic Banquet, or Lord's Supper. We have seen that ideally it is attended by the High Priest, or priestly Messiah, his Davidic counterpart, and the whole Congregation of Israel under their elders and sages. That Jesus was well acquainted with the idea has long been recognized, not only through his parables of the Banquet but in the incidents of crowd-feeding by the Sea of Galilee, which are but an earthly anticipation of the Messianic Feast. The Last Supper of Jesus is again clearly connected in his mind with the coming heavenly Banquet:

> for I say unto you, I will not drink from henceforth of the fruit of the vine until the Kingdom of God shall come . . . I appoint unto you a kingdom, even as my Father appointed unto me, that ye may eat and drink at my table in my kingdom; and ye shall sit on thrones judging the twelve tribes of Israel (Luke xxii. 18, 29–30).

As most probably for the Qumran Sect, this Last Supper, according to a strong tradition, was a Passover ceremony, and again Mlle Jaubert has put forward a good case for resolving some of the difficulties presented by the apparent contradiction in chronology between the Synoptists and the Fourth Gospel by suggesting that the former, and presumably Jesus, used the old priestly calendar whilst John is referring to the legal system. The Qumran Covenanters would have been celebrating their Passover on the Tuesday night, and she suggests, with the support of a tradition contained in the third century *Didascalia,* that it was then that Jesus held his Last Supper with his disciples, three days before his crucifixion and the orthodox observance of the Passover.

Another curious point of the gospel narrative appears in a revealing light through the Qumran *Manual.* Luke records that after the Supper

> there arose a contention among them which of them is accounted to be the greatest (xxii. 24).

Now in the *Manual,* the seating and serving of the

participants of the Messianic Banquet was strictly according to their respective ranks in the kingdom. If Jesus and His disciples are observing this Qumran ritual, the disputing of the twelve about precedence is clearly occasioned by their order of seating, not as a matter of petty pride, but because their position in the heavenly kingdom was concerned. Although we read that Jesus sharply rebukes this preoccupation with rank, and thus apparently upsets the established form of ritual, the Lucan account goes on then to his promise of a place at the true Messianic Feast, and of the twelve thrones in the new Kingdom.

CHAPTER TWELVE

THE MESSIANIC CONCEPTIONS OF QUMRAN AND THE EARLY CHURCH

IN the preceding pages, we have noted correspondences between the Qumran Sect and the Church in matters of order, discipline, religious doctrines, use of Scripture, and even ritual. They are too close and too varied to be accidental, and must, at least, point to a common religious background. But the question of there being an even closer affinity between them must hinge largely on their respective expectations concerning the Messiah. If it could be shown that their hopes in this respect were mutually exclusive, then no real contact, such as the acceptance by one of the members of the other, would be likely. But we shall see that this is not necessarily so.

The Qumran Sect looked to the coming of a Priestly Messiah, whom they call 'Teacher of Righteousness' and 'Interpreter of the Law'. The fact that these are precisely the terms they apply to the priestly founder of the Sect supports the idea that it was none other than their resurrected Teacher who would lead the theocratic community of the New Israel in the Last Days. Furthermore, a fragmentary commentary on Hosea refers to the Lion of Wrath (*kᵉphīr haḥarôn*), which we have seen meant the persecutor of the Teacher, Alexander Jannaeus, and directly underneath, to the Last Priest (*kôhēn hā'aḥᵃrôn*), who would 'stretch forth his hand to smite Ephraim', the pseudonym used elsewhere for the Sect's enemies in Jerusalem. The Lion and the Priest are clearly connected here by the play on their names, and since the Last Priest (or Priest of the

End) could only refer to the Messiah, the conclusion that the Lion's victim and the coming High Priest are one and the same person seems almost inescapable. Again, the Sect seem to have expected that the Last Days would see the punishment of the Wicked Priest and the vindication of the Teacher, both long since dead. They must therefore have looked forward to a general resurrection to judgement of the type envisaged in Daniel and the New Testament.

It seems that the triumphal march of the Messiah to Jerusalem was expected to begin from the vicinity of Qumran, since a commentary on Isaiah, which is concerned mainly with eschatalogical events, speaks of 'his going up from the Vale of Achor' to the Holy City in the last days, following the promulgation of a great decree, apparently calling the faithful to the point of assembly. This Vale of Achor is certainly to be identified with the modern Buqei'a, lying between Qumran and Jerusalem, and the substitution by our commentary of the exact Hebrew equivalent of the modern Arabic, *biq'ah* 'valley' for the biblical *'ēmeq,* may not be without significance. It appears from other references that the Sect may have regarded this area as of special importance for Israel's history, and a further hint towards the reason for their choice of Qumran for their home may possibly be found in the words of Hosea:

> Therefore, behold, I will allure her, and bring her into the wilderness, and speak comfortably unto her. And I will give her her vineyards from thence, and the valley of Achor for a door of hope: and she shall make answer there, as in the days of her youth, and as in the day when she came out of the land of Egypt (ii. 14–15).

The Buqei'a, to which one may climb even to-day from Qumran on a well-marked path over the cliffs at the head of the Wady (pl. 38), was thus to the Sect the 'door of hope', the gateway to the New Jerusalem, the end of another forty years' wandering in the wilderness and the promise of a new, spiritual Canaan at the end of time.

But this new Kingdom was essentially a holy institution, a congregation of saints devoted to the service of God and the study of His Law. To the Covenanters, the onset of the new order would mean a continuation of the pious existence they were then leading, for the whole idea of their present way of life was that it should be a rehearsal of the messianic age. But, then, their communion with God would be complete, for any difficulties in the interpretation of the Law, or questions concerning their way of life, could be referred to their messianic Teacher of Righteousness, the perfect mediator between Man and God.

This, then, was the priestly Messiah, but it is now clear that along with him they expected the appearance of another, lay, Anointed One, a Prince of the line of David. It is not, perhaps, surprising that it was some time before scholars realized that phrases like 'the Messiah of Aaron and Israel' in Qumran literature, actually meant 'the Messiah of Aaron *and the Messiah* of Israel', many having taken the one instance where we find the plural 'the Messiahs of Aaron and Israel' as a scribal error, or the like.

However, once the idea of two Messiahs had been considered at all feasible, correspondences were found in Jewish thought both before and after the Qumran period, which showed that the idea was not, after all, so very unique. The origins seem to go back to the breaking down of the old theocracy of Israel, when both secular and spiritual power was in the hands of the High Priest. There arose a secular political régime, often in conflict with the religious interests of the nation and the two arms of government drew farther and farther apart. With the patterning of the messianic on the temporal order, the need for both sides to be represented in the new era was envisaged, and even as early as the end of the sixth century, we see both the Aaronic High Priest and the Davidic prince referred to as 'the anointed', literally 'sons of oil' (Zechariah iv. 14). With the loss of independence, the title of King naturally lapsed, and it was not until Hasmonean times that the two offices were united by the High Priest's adoption of the title of King, an act of usurpation which shocked the pious Israelite of the time.

However, the idea of the dual messianic office continued at least until the time of the Second Revolt (A.D. 132–5), for the coins of that time speak of El'azar the High Priest, side by side with Shim'on bar Kochebah, the Prince of Israel.

We have already seen that at the Messianic Banquet described in the *Manual,* both the High Priest and the Messiah of Israel are mentioned, and another document refers to them both as arising together at the end of time. The Davidic Messiah is really a war leader and judge, and in the blessing upon him recorded in the *Manual,* it is said that

> he will renew for Him the Covenant of the Community (charging him) to established the kingdom of His people for ev[er, to judge the poor justly, and] to reprove with e[quity the hum]ble of the land, to walk before Him in perfection, in all the ways of [. . .], and to restore His [holy all]iance [in] the time of distress with all those who seek [Him. May] the Lord li[ft th]ee up to an everlasting height like a fortified tower on a high wall, that thou [mightest smite the peoples] with the might of thy [mouth], with thy sceptre devastate the land, and with the breath of thy lips kill the wick[ed, armed with the spirit of cou]nsel and everlasting might, the spirit of knowledge, and the fear of God. And righteousness shall be the girdle [of thy loins, and fai]th the belt of thy reins. [And] may He make thy horns of iron and thy hooves of brass to gore like a young bu[ll . . . and tread down the peop]les like the mire of the streets. For God has established thee as a sceptre over rulers. Bef[ore thee shall they come and do obeisance, and all the nat]ions will serve thee, and by His holy name He will strengthen thee. And thou shalt be like a l[ion . . .] prey with none to resto[re], and thy [mess]engers will spread over [the face of the earth . . .

The Davidic Messiah, then, is the warrior of God, the holy instrument by which He will restore the kingdom of His people, and protect the pious poor who seek to know Him. And it is with this lay Messiah that we may expect to find correspondences with Christian ideas. Like the

Qumran Messiah, Jesus was expected to 'kill the wicked with the breath of his lips' (cp. 2 Thessalonians ii. 8), and the inscription which the soldiers nailed above his cross should, perhaps, better have read 'Prince of Israel', than 'King of the Jews', for the former is the title of the Qumran Messiah, as it was applied later on to the messianic leader of the Second Jewish Revolt, Bar Kochebah. To both the Qumran Messiah and to Jesus was applied the prophecy of Isaiah 11, the 'shoot out of the stock of Jesse', and the 'Prophet' prophecy of Deuteronomy xviii. 18 is found in the messianic 'testimonies' document from Qumran as well as the New Testament. The Covenanters saw the coming of their 'shoot of David' as ordained for the salvation of Israel, and we remember that it was precisely for this that Jesus received his name (Matthew i. 21).

It is stated in the order of the Messianic Banquet that God would 'beget' the Davidic Messiah. It is true that this word could conceivably have been used here with the weakened sense of 'produce' or the like, or it could, as the editors suggest, be a scribal error for 'lead'; but, taken with the Sect's application of the prophecy in 2 Samuel vii:

> I will establish the throne of his kingdom for ever.
> I will be his father, and he shall be my son

to their Davidic Messiah, just as the Church did for Jesus, it is not impossible that we have in this phrase a contributory factor to the Church's conception of 'the only-begotten of the Father'.

When discussing the Sectarian and New Testament use of Scripture, we noted that the prophecy of Zechariah ix. 9, about the king riding on an ass, was used of Jesus' entry into Jerusalem on Palm Sunday. Now this passage in Zechariah is clearly dependent upon a messianic interpretation of Genesis xlix. 10–11, about the Lion of Judah, referred to often in the book of Revelation. Again, this Genesis passage is quoted and given a messianic significance in a Qumran document, where, instead of 'until Shiloh come', it has 'until the Messiah of Righteousness come', and goes on to say that this refers to the 'shoot of David', to whose seed would be given the kingdom of his people. Similarly, to the coming of this Messiah, a Qumran writer refers the fulfilment of the prophecy of Amos:

> In that day I will raise up the tabernacle of David that is fallen (ix. 11).

quoted by James the Apostle (Acts xv. 16).

But it is important to realize that, in all things, the Priestly Messiah of Qumran was expected to take precedence over his lay counterpart. This is amply demonstrated in the order for the Messianic Banquet, where the Priests must be seated before the Davidic Messiah may enter with his followers. Nobody must touch the wine and bread before the Priest has laid his hands upon it and distributed it to his priests. Only then may the Davidic Messiah do the same for his company of laymen.

There seems to be nothing which would preclude the acceptance by the Qumran Sect of Jesus as the expected Messiah of David's line. Certainly, the idea of the Messiah undergoing a baptism of suffering before his death and expected resurrection would have been in no way repugnant to the Sectarian. But how long the disciples would have accepted a subordinate position in the messianic order for their own Master is a different matter. Certainly, by the time of writing of the Epistle to the Hebrews, Jesus has been placed in the role of the priestly Messiah, and the author is having not a little difficulty in explaining how Jesus, born of the line of David, a non-priestly family, could undertake these duties:

> For the priesthood being changed, there is made of necessity a change also of the law. For he of whom these things are said belongeth to another tribe, from which no man hath given attendance at the altar. For it is evident that our Lord hath sprung out of Judah; as to which tribe Moses spake nothing concerning priests (vii. 12–14).

He therefore concludes that Jesus, the Davidic Messiah, has been given a special priesthood of a unique order, surpassing that of the old Aaronic line, and patterned after the ancient priest-king, Melchizedek. In Jesus, the various functions of both Messiahs have been combined.

CHAPTER THIRTEEN

THE QUMRAN SECT AND JESUS

In the last chapter we saw that there was nothing formally incompatible in the messianic expectations of the Qumran Sect and the Christian Messiah. It remains now to consider how far Jesus himself was influenced by Qumran teaching. The difficulty, however, with this, as with any other study of Jesus' life and thought, is that we are dependent entirely on the records of the New Testament which, in their present form, cannot be claimed to represent with certainty the standpoint of the first Jewish-Christians of Jerusalem. The fact is that the Church cannot offer first-hand manuscripts of its records of anything like the antiquity of the documents from Qumran, although that is not to say, of course, that the New Testament does not preserve traditions going back to the very earliest days. The difficulty is to find an objective yard-stick with which this 'original' material might be measured. However, certain essential features of Jesus' life do seem to stand out clearly.

For upwards of thirty years Jesus remained at his home in Nazareth. It seems to have been the stories of the strange and compelling preacher of the Jordan valley which first brought him south to Judaea. Whatever may have been his previous ideas of his life's mission, it was the fiery urgency of the Baptist's message which was the starting point of Jesus' public ministry. Soon after his baptism at John's hands, he withdrew into the desert nearby and began a period of fasting and prayer which lasted, we are told, forty days. This desert withdrawal is the key to the whole life and teaching of Jesus, and begins our first concrete correspondence with the Qumran Community. Just as their withdrawal to the desert was in conscious imitation of the first forty years' wandering by the Israelites in the deserts of

Sinai, so Jesus for the token period of forty days underwent the preparatory period before his appearance as Messiah. He, just like the Qumran Community, is identifying himself with the True Israel, and like the Sect is voluntarily undergoing sufferings through which alone the atonement for the world's sins can be accomplished. For Jesus, as for the Covenanters, the 'last days' had come, and the cosmic battle of the Spirits is drawing to the climax. As the Sect saw itself as a pregnant woman giving birth to a Messiah through her travail, so Jesus sees himself born out of the sufferings of his people, and suffering with them. All are his kin,

> Behold, my mother and my brethren!

and in this sense of identification of himself with the righteous remnant, he takes upon himself the character of the Suffering Servant of Isaiah. On him will be laid the iniquity of the world, he will bear its griefs and carry its sorrows, and through his remaining firm in the face of the onslaughts of the Devil, he will usher in the new Age and God's Kingdom. Thus the Qumran Sect saw itself purified and chosen 'to atone for the land', and they spent their time resisting the wiles of the Evil One by which he would snare them into impurity and make them stumble from righteousness.

The Devil tempted Jesus in the desert with 'the authority of kingdoms and their glory', but he saw his work as beginning with the battle of the Spirits within him, the tearing of his own soul as he faced alone the world's battle of Good against Evil. Only when that war had been won could he take on himself the cloak of the kingly Messiah and come 'in clouds with great power and glory'. It is important, I think, to realize that when Jesus resisted this temptation in the wilderness, he was not, as is so often said, rejecting the contemporary idea of messiahship; he was rather adding to it its most vital part.

And so, in the Judaean desert, perhaps only a mile or two from Qumran itself, Jesus threw down his challenge to the Devil and his forces, in the firm belief that he was fighting not only his own battle, for which he was more than equipped, but that of all mankind. From then on, every sin man committed, every hurt inflicted on his neighbour, every failing in his love for God, was Jesus' responsibility, and by his suffering would man be purified and the powers of darkness finally defeated. The coming of the Kingdom depended on him, the Messiah, and his was a baptism none could envy, 'and how was he constrained until it be accomplished'.

Jesus' main message when he returned from the desert was that of the nearness of the end and the urgency of the moment:

> The time is fulfilled, and the Kingdom of God is at hand.

The final combat which men now faced would be most terrible; Satan and his forces of darkness would fight the more ferociously now as the end approached, desperately anxious to claim men's souls. Many would be lost in the final cataclysm, and terrible pictures of the Last Days are drawn for us in the thirteenth chapter of St Mark's Gospel, matched in intensity only by those in the Qumran writings. But while there was time every soul who would listen must be saved. If, at the end of the Galilean ministry, Jesus' words show signs of disappointment, almost resignation, it is not because he now saw an ignominious death before him, for that had been there from the beginning, an essential part of his high office. What grieved him was Man's obstinacy in the face of impending doom. He would have taken so many more of his fellow men under his wing and saved them from the horrors to come had they only listened, and now the end was at hand and little time remained.

Jesus is often pictured to us as a good and kindly man, whose main mission on earth was to go about feeding the hungry and healing the sick. But this is less than the truth. First and foremost, Jesus was the herald of the new Kingdom, giving warning of the terrible wrath to come. His feeding of the thousands was, as we have seen, a rehearsal of the Messianic Banquet, his healing acts demonstrations of the victory of Light over Darkness, signs of the ultimate victory of the Spirit of Truth over Satan:

> I beheld Satan fallen as lightning from heaven.

Indeed, a close reading of the Gospels will show that there was very little that Jesus said and did which did not bear directly on this battle of the heavens and the coming of the Kingdom. Similarly, a great deal of the literature from Qumran is concerned almost entirely with this hope of salvation and the endurance of the time of wickedness which must precede it.

Jesus seems to have shared the Qumran Sect's contempt for the religious leaders in Jerusalem. His conflicts with the Scribes and Pharisees appear throughout the Gospels, and his prime charge against them is the one of hypocrisy. This sin seemed the most terrible to Jesus since it blinded a man to his own failings and thus gave him a false estimate of his position in the fight with the Devil. Thieves and harlots Jesus could abide and even love, but stiff-necked, self-righteous men he could never tolerate, and seeing about him sheep needing true shepherds, soon to be caught up in this awful maelstrom of apocalyptic events, his fury at the time-serving clergy sometimes broke all bonds and he spits his condemnation at those who neglect their sacred trust.

Yet these Pharisees were descendants of the Hasidim of Maccabean times, the spiritual forebears of the Qumran Sectarians themselves. Where had their paths divided, leading the one to the condemned hypocrisy and the other to sound the very depths of sincere religious communion? Jesus would probably have answered that the Pharisees had come to terms with Mammon, had contented themselves with the outward observance of the Law and neglected the real issues within the heart of Man. It is not true that they had left the people to their own devices whilst they made sure of their own salvation. In fact, one of the arguments of the Sadducees against them was that they had been too zealous in their efforts at ruling other people's lives, adding to the Law hundreds of ordinances for daily life which had no basis in Scripture. It was rather that their cherished legalism had led them farther and farther away from the main issues involved, the war between the powers of darkness and the forces of light. They seemed to have contented themselves with believing that if the secular authorities would only give them peace and quiet in which to perform their meticulous purity regulations for themselves and their charges, they could meet their political enemies half-way, supporting their 'reforms' and condoning their crimes. Modern parallels jump too readily to mind. The Qumran sectarians called these people 'Seekers after Smooth Things', and yet to our mind their painstaking efforts to avoid 'contamination' from ritual uncleanliness would seem to have made their lives anything but smooth. The real truth as the Covenanters and Jesus saw it was that the sacrifice of energy and time in following an involved ritual is as nothing compared with the wrestling of moral victory from the power of personal sin. It may be that the latter depends to some extent on the discipline enjoined by the former, but then ritual takes its place as but a means to an end; the Pharisees had made it an end in itself.

Of course, Jesus is much more of a flesh-and-blood character than the Qumran Teacher could ever be. This is largely due to the more complete records we possess of Jesus' life and ministry, thanks mainly to the need for this type of historical record in the Church's proselytizing of the Graeco-Roman world. As we have seen, the nearest Qumran approaches to such 'Gospels' are the biblical commentaries, which, from the point of view of detail and objectivity, leave much to be desired by the historian. But there is another fundamental difference. The Qumran Sect was a monastic community, cut off from their fellow-men, and seeking first ritual purity and the simple life. All things not considered essential to this sort of existence they discarded, believing that sacrifices made then would be amply rewarded in the life to come. They were also essentially a priestly community, founded by priests, and, although admitting a lay element, largely ruled by priests. But Jesus was a layman, and his work took him mainly among ordinary folk in the towns and villages of Palestine. His parables are masterpieces of homely preaching, directed towards a peasant community whose manner of living is reflected in every word. Very different is the apocalyptic imagery of the Qumran literature, and it rings as strange in our ears as that of the books of Daniel and Revelation, which stand in exactly the same tradition. We feel more at home with Jesus' parables, but basically the message is the same.

Of more importance is the question of how to explain the common ground between Jesus and a monastic community. There is no evidence that he was ever a member of this body, and, indeed, since his life was mostly spent in Nazareth, such a close connexion is highly improbable. There is another, more likely solution.

The ancient historian tells us that next to the Pharisees and Sadducees, there existed a third Jewish Sect called the *Essenes*, the spiritual successors, as we have seen, of the Hasidim of Maccabean times. From various sources we are able to gather quite a deal of information about these people and their ideas, although as some of it seems directly contradictory, not too much reliance should be placed on matters of detail. However, it does seem certain that they possessed a monastic settlement by the Dead Sea, 'above En Geddi', in a position which corresponds exactly with that of our Qumran monastery. Pliny further describes these people as unique of their kind, living without money and as celibates, maintaining their numbers by accepting new members who turn in disgust from the world and seek to share their way of life. Their basic doctrines and many of their institutions are strikingly similar to those of the Qumran Sect, and correspondences are to be found in their novitiate, baptism, initiatory oath, common meals, spurning of the world's riches, humility, continence, semi-determinism, angelology, doctrines of heavenly rewards and hell fire; their regard for the writings of the prophets as for the

Law, allegorical exegesis, and the sanctity of their own sectarian works. But for our immediate problem, the most important fact we learn is that there existed a kind of 'Third Order' of these people, living pious lives of love and humility in the towns and villages of Palestine. Apart from those who practised celibacy, there were others who married and lived normal family lives, except that marital intercourse was indulged in only in so far as it was necessary to beget children.

Widespread as they were, it seems reasonable to assume that Jesus was acquainted with such people, and that his moral teaching owed much to their influence, a point, perhaps, we should remember before dragging all his words out of their context and applying them automatically to our own day and situation. Be that as it may, here is a very possible means of access to Qumran ideas for Jesus, if we are to see both groups as part of the same religious movement. Furthermore, it seems very likely that the Jewish-Christian Church won its first adherents from the Essenes, and this, again, would account for its possession of so much Qumran thought, and, perhaps, literature. It is possible that the 'great company of priests' who were 'obedient to the faith', mentioned in Acts vi. 7, included at least part of the spiritual leadership of this movement. But if this be so, we can be sure that the faith to which they were obedient was founded more on those elements common to Qumran and the Jerusalem Church, than on the characteristic Pauline Christianity which eventually won over the Graeco-Roman world.

For the faith which broke through the bounds of Judaism and became a living fount of inspiration for the western world was far removed from Qumran Judaism. Despite the mention of the 'son-ship' of the Davidic Messiah in Qumran literature, nothing found there approaches the Christology of Paul. The whole concept of the God-Man, readily acceptable to the Greek, would have been as abhorrent to the Covenanter then as it is to the Jew and Muslim to-day. Again, a Gospel of salvation for the Gentile would have been equally difficult for the Covenanter, whose future Kingdom was strictly a Jewish foundation. But at the heart there was an even greater difference. For Paul the whole of his faith hinged on an historical Resurrection of Jesus. For him the Messiah had come, been put to death, and had risen again, and the way of the believer to salvation was by faith in this risen Lord. The Covenanters were presumably still waiting for the Resurrection of their Master when they were swept away, and, like the Jewish-Christian community itself, became extinct. But by then the basic elements of their faith had been given a far wider setting, and a significance for all mankind.

APPENDIX I

JOHN THE BAPTIST

To most people the association of the River Jordan, baptism and the call to repentance brings to mind most vividly the figure of John the Baptist. Marked off from his youth for the ascetic life of a prophet, John remained in the deserts of Judaea until 'the time of his showing unto Israel'. His wild, unkempt appearance, his uncompromising call to repentance, and his fanatical assurance of the nearness of the Day of Judgement, made a particular appeal to the people when he finally began his public ministry. He cared for no man and condemned hypocrisy and complacency wherever he found it, to the delight of the ordinary man who had suffered enough from both in the priesthood. There seems to have grown up around him a band of admirers who were later inclined to ascribe to him a messianic role, which, according to the Fourth Gospel, he was most anxious to deny. He was but a messenger,

> the voice of one crying in the wilderness,
> Make straight the way of the Lord.

John's baptism was for the remission of sins, but that remission depended on a genuine showing of the fruits of repentance, after which alone could the suppliant be purified in the flesh with water. Even this was a preparatory ritual only, for the days were coming when the Messiah himself would baptize, not with water, but

> with the Holy Spirit and with fire.

Indeed, the eschatological process had already begun,

> even now the axe is laid unto the root of the trees,

and thoughts of personal wealth and prestige could be put aside for ever. Now was the time to share one's worldly goods, to live honestly, and in quiet expectation of the end.

The Qumran Community quoted the same Isaianic passage to describe their own work of preparation, which was to study the Law and abide by the teachings of Moses and the prophets. They also demanded true repentance before baptism, and likewise promised a further cleansing by God

> through the Holy Spirit . . . sprinkling upon him a Spirit of Truth as purifying water.

As we know, the Sect believed in the approach of the Day of Visitation and that this period of preparation would not allow of the accumulation of personal wealth, and they practised communal ownership of property.

Yet for all the similarities in their respective teachings, John was clearly at this time not of the Qumran Community. His mixing with the common man and thus separation from the 'Purity of the Many' would make his continued membership of the Community impossible. Theirs was no evangelistic call to mankind, but an esoteric Community of the Elect. Whilst others could join, it was only after a rigorous period of self-denial and probation. It does appear, however, that John belonged to the Essene movement, and correspondences with Qumran doctrine could easily be explained on the basis of their possessing many ideas and documents which were common to the Essene Sect as a whole. One interesting suggestion has been advanced that John had been adopted by the Qumran Sect as a boy, and this would certainly account for his being in the deserts at such an early age. We know from Josephus that some branches of the Essenes eschewed marriage, and to keep up their number adopted other people's children

> whilst yet pliable and docile, and regarded them as their kin and moulded them in accordance with their own principles.

As the son of a priest he would have been welcomed by such a Community and probably marked out for a leading role in the Sect. When we meet him he is no longer a member, which may suggest expulsion or voluntary resignation, perhaps when he received this overwhelming conviction of the need to take his message to the common people. We are told that besides his wearing of only the simplest garments, he ate only honey and locusts, both of which are mentioned in the food laws at the end of the Damascus Document. This again may indicate that the food he was able to eat was strictly limited owing to his purity vows taken in the Community.

Whether this theory be in accordance with the facts or not, it is certain that John the Baptist and his disciples exercised a very considerable influence on Jesus and the Church, and it is equally certain that much of John's message finds its parallels in Qumran teaching.

APPENDIX II

OTHER CAVE DISCOVERIES OF HISTORY AND AFFILIATIONS WITH THE QUMRAN SECT

At some time about the beginning of the ninth century of our era, a Syrian Metropolitan of Seleucia, Timotheus, writing to his superior, recounted an incident which had been told him by some Jewish proselytes from Jerusalem. It seems that, about ten years before, an Arab shepherd boy had been searching for a lost animal near Jericho and had stumbled upon a cave, and, climbing in, had discovered some ancient scrolls. He had told some Jews in Jerusalem who went down and cleared many more scrolls, finding that they were written in Hebrew and in an old script, and contained biblical and other works. Timotheus suggested that the cache had been placed there by Jeremiah and Baruch before the Exile, which may indicate that his informants had told him that the scrolls had been found in jars, with which he had connected the 'earthen vessel' of Jeremiah xxxii. 14. In any case, Timotheus says that he himself was most interested in whether these scrolls contained Old Testament texts in the variant forms in which they appear in the New Testament, but save for hearing that they were so represented in the scrolls, he was unable to gain further information.

We have already seen in Chapter 7 that Karaite and Muslim writers of the tenth-twelfth centuries were speaking of a Cave Sect, so called because their documents had been discovered in a cave, and we noted that the calendar used by this sect seems to correspond with that favoured by the Qumran Covenanters and found in the book of Jubilees.

Furthermore, the *Damascus Document*, of which we have had occasion to speak previously, was first known to modern scholarship in medieval copies found at the end of the last century in an ancient Karaite synagogue in Cairo. Although dated palaeographically to the tenth and twelfth centuries A.D., it was soon recognized that their contents stemmed from a very much earlier period, and the discovery of fragmentary copies in the Qumran caves occasioned no great surprise. But scholars have noted that Karaite literature of the ninth and tenth centuries begins to show remarkable correspondences with Qumran writings. At this time, words and expressions previously absent from the literature of this Jewish sect over the preceding centuries begin to appear. For example, the title 'Teacher of Righteousness' does not appear before the ninth-century commentary on Joel by an author of the Sect. Furthermore, from the second half of the ninth century until the tenth, the underlying antagonism between the Karaite sect of Jews and the orthodox Rabbanites suddenly flares up in a new burst of polemic activity. There are constant references to the 'Zadokite' sect and its doctrine in the literature of this period, and the writings of the group appear to have had a wide circulation, being 'well known among the people', according to a Karaite author. Furthermore, the Rabbanites of Jerusalem of the tenth century themselves began to adopt religious practices which were by no means the custom in Talmudic circles. Thus they became partly vegetarians, avoided cooked food, olive oil, honey, and, indeed, any food likely to contain 'crawling things' or other impurities. They applied strictly the law of levitical purity, not allowing the marriage with a niece or stepsister. Most interestingly, in view of what we have said about the calendar, they began to duplicate the observation of religious festivals, fixing the one set by observation and the other by the old traditional system of calendation. The tenth-century Karaite author who tells us this says that they borrowed these practices from his own sect. Certainly many of the new customs are to be found promoted in Karaite writings, and some of the dietary restrictions and levitical laws of purity approximate to what we find in the legal section of the *Damascus Document*.

All these lines of evidence leave little doubt that at the end of the ninth century a startling discovery of manuscripts, which bear many important resemblances to those from the Qumran library, was made similarly in a cave near Jericho. The documents must have been assiduously copied and taken into circulation, with a considerable effect on all those who came into contact with them. The Karaites seem to have found in them much which accorded with their own ideals, which might throw some interesting new light on the origins of this important Jewish sectarian movement. But even the orthodox Rabbanites seem to have recognized a note of authority in these writings which made them adopt a double calendar and unfamiliar food and purity laws.

APPENDIX III

MURABBA'AT

IT was not until January 1952 that an official excavation of the Murabba'at caves (Chapter 2) was possible, and once more the Jordanian Department of Antiquities under Gerald Harding, and the French School of Archaeology led by Father De Vaux undertook the task. The main difficulty of this excavation was that of supplies, since the rains were still falling and stores had to be brought by mule and donkey the whole seven-hour march from Bethlehem as far as the cliffs in which the caves were situated, and then down the last dizzy slopes on human backs.

The Wady Murabba'at or Darajeh is a great gorge, starting under the name of Wady Ta'amireh, east of Bethlehem, almost sheer on its north side and sloping steeply on the south, until, as it enters the Dead Sea, the sides are almost vertical (see map on p. 10). The caves are on the north side of the gorge, at this point some eight hundred feet deep, and about eighteen miles south-east of Jerusalem and eleven miles south of the First Cave of Qumran, as the crow flies. Three of them stand together in the vertical cliff face, and the fourth is about eight hundred feet to the east. Running along the foot of the cliff is a narrow rock ledge about eight feet wide, and on this the party pitched their tents. Whilst most convenient for the work, this spot lost some of its attractiveness when it rained, as the water streaming down the slope was apt to loosen large rocks *en route* and send them crashing into the camp. One member had left his tent only a few minutes before a boulder crashed through the roof and smashed into his pillow. The next night he spent in the cave.

Cave One is really a long tunnel running into the mountain side for about two hundred feet and stands some twenty feet high and the same wide. The ceiling had collapsed in the remote past, and the first levels of occupation were found on top of the collapsed stones. The roof of the Second Cave, however, had only partially collapsed, almost completely blocking the doorway (pl. 4), so that the first task was to break up the huge boulders and roll them down the cliff face. Unfortunately, the primitive delight which the sight of large rocks crashing their way down hundreds of feet of vertical mountain side usually engenders in the hearts of children and archaeologists, was somewhat tempered by the knowledge that all the noise going on might shift the remainder of the roof of the cave, hanging precariously above the workers. Every stroke of the foreman's hammer as it crashed into the large slabs of rock, therefore, made the party look anxiously aloft, ready to spring to safety at any sign of movement.

If these hazards were not enough, it soon became evident as the men cleared away the largest boulders that the excavators would have to include pot-holing among their activities, for the narrow crevices revealed led far down into the bowels of the mountain. The most persistent difficulty of the early days, however, revealed itself within the first ten minutes of their beginning work. So much of the fine grey dust was kicked up in that time by the workmen that all the pressure lamps became clogged and went out. The team had to fall back on the smoking paraffin flares which the Bedouin had been using. The atmosphere soon became almost unbreathable, but at least there was a murky light to work by.

It was with one of these flares that Harding and a Ta'amireh workman undertook their first burrowing expedition. The workman went in front with the torch and Harding crawled behind, half choked by the fumes of the oil and the dust raised by his companion. However they made fair progress for about fifty feet when suddenly both flare and bearer disappeared. One moment the Bedouin was there raising clouds of dust behind him and the next he was gone, leaving Jordan's Director of Antiquities completely in the dark, scared, as he freely admits, out of his wits and one workman in Sheol. However, after a little while a voice cried to Allah out of the depths, the flare was relit and the son of the desert climbed out of the pit into which he had fallen, apparently none the worse for his adventure. Later on the lighting situation was saved, thanks to the ready assistance of the Arab Legion who supplied a portable generator for the use of the expedition. But even that raised grave difficulties, for the heavy parts had to be carried down to the scene of operations on human backs, down tracks which even the loaded mules would not attempt. On another occasion, in the Third Cave, investigation disclosed a great crack in the rock at the back of the cave going down into the depths of the mountain. The Bedouin said that one of their number had already explored it, but to be sure, the foreman of Harding's party, one Hasan Awad, probably the best archaeological foreman in Jordan, volunteered to go down into the crevice on a rope himself. The opening was only two and a half feet wide, and some way down was an even narrower chimney through which he could barely squeeze. Altogether he dropped some fifty feet before landing on a sandy floor, which bore traces of the earlier visit by the Bedouin but nothing of archaeological value. The haul up was a nightmare for all concerned, as, having no pulleys, the party at the surface had to haul Hasan up, inch by inch, trusting that the rope would not break or be cut by a sharp projection of rock. The half an hour that it took to bring him to the surface seemed like half a day, and the bravery displayed by this man cannot be accounted too highly. Its recounting here may serve to underline the tremendous difficulties under which these archaeologists were working here and in Qumran to the north, and should demonstrate something of the cost at which these priceless Dead Sea Scrolls were won.

At the front of the first cave was a large Roman cistern, carefully lined with plaster, with steps leading down into it, and, in front, a small settling tank. How the water was led into it remains a mystery. The cistern had once been covered, the roof constructed corbel fashion with large flat stones after the fashion of the many such Roman cisterns to be found all along the route to Bethlehem. Long after the rains have ceased the Bedouin can find water in them for themselves and their flocks.

But deeper excavations showed that these caves had been used by man long before the time of the Romans. In all of them sherds were found dating from the Chalcolithic period, about 4000–3000 B.C. In Cave Two, the purely chalcolithic stratum was found sealed by the rocks which obstructed the entrance, and in the lower galleries was found the same layer, about fourteen inches thick, giving directly on to virgin soil, and itself covered by a layer almost as thick of red earth and stones before the debris of later occupations. Flint tools were found in this layer, sickle and other blades, javelin heads, a large scraper, etc., as well as polishers, pierced buttons, and a flat ring of very hard red limestone. There were bone instruments like awls and pointed blades, but the most incredible discoveries in this six-thousand-year-old layer were the wooden objects. These included a donkey goad, which, had the archaeologists not been there when it was discovered, they might have thought had been cut only the day before by the workmen, and a perfectly preserved haft of an adze, with its polished handle and even the leather thongs for holding the flint blade in position, all in perfect order (pl. 6). This wonderful state of preservation is due, of course, to the complete protection the inmost recesses of these caves enjoy from the elements and the drying influence of the terrific heat in this area for many months in the year.

Also from Cave Two were discovered the remains of a Middle Bronze Age settlement, both in the upper chamber and in the galleries. Besides the pottery were found two bronze needles and a small alabaster vase. Absolute evidence for dating is happily provided by a scarab decorated with the classical motifs of the Hyksos period. No evidence of a long occupation was forthcoming, but it could mean that in the second part of the Middle Bronze Age, towards the eighteenth and seventeenth centuries, a small human group, or even a few individuals, sojourned in this cave. Probably then, as certainly in later times, these caves offered a refuge from danger during troubled times.

Caves One, Two, and Three all yielded remains of Iron Age occupation, pottery indicating habitation between the eighth and seventh centuries B.C. But the use of the caves was most intense in the Roman period, particularly in the first two caves. Pottery, though fragmentary, was abundant and clearly Roman, and the lamps can be dated quite precisely to the end of the second century of our era. Many metal objects were found, the heads of picks and javelins, generally of bronze, arrow heads of iron, one in the laurel leaf form, and many with three edges. Among the utensils were knives, one of which had its handle of wood quite intact, a sickle, nails, a spatula, a hook, needles of different shapes, and an angular key. Wooden objects were plentiful and included bowls and plates of turned wood, combs, buttons, and spoons. There was a great variety of fabrics, mostly the remains of clothing, often very patched but delicately embroidered. Leather remains included sandals and other equipment. Again evidence was forthcoming for a definite dating of this occupation, for a score of coins appeared, the most numerous being those of the Second Jewish Revolt of A.D. 132–5.

The written documents came almost entirely from the Second Cave. A few are fairly well preserved, but most had suffered from the depredations of visiting animals, human and otherwise, and particularly in the activities of rats who, with a regrettable lack of appreciation of true values, had used the precious leather and papyrus manuscripts as linings for their nests. In fact, the excavation developed into a hunt for rats' nests, since each one was almost sure to produce remnants of a written document or two. Another contributory factor in the denudation of written material was that the later habitation by birds and small animals of the caves over hundreds of years had resulted in an abundant supply of guano which the Bedouin had for years been collecting and selling in Bethlehem. It is not at all improbable, as Father De Vaux points out, that the Jewish orange groves near Bethlehem were fertilized with priceless ancient manuscripts written by their forefathers!

The most amazing documentary find of this excavation was that of a papyrus palimpsest written in a very ancient Hebrew script which palaeographically can be estimated to precede the writing on the sixth-century Lachish ostraca, and which Father Milik would put to the eighth century B.C. It is certainly an undreamed of discovery for Palestine. If this area can produce a papyrus document of such an age, what future wonders may it yet turn up from the documentarily barren period of the Hebrew kings? The superimposed text seems to be a list of names accompanied by signs, some certainly numerals. The text below is very defaced, but one can see the formula of salutation which would precede a letter.

There are a number of ostraca, nearly all inscribed in Hebrew, rarely in Greek. Many are just the letters of a name, but one large fragment of a jar bears the first part of the Hebrew alphabet, each letter being written twice. There are Greek papyri, two of them marriage contracts or the like. One is very fragmentary, but bears the words 'gift' and 'inheritance', whilst the other is better preserved and quite large, about 12 in. by 6 in. It seems to treat of the reconciliation of a couple whose names are Elias and Salome. Several place names are mentioned, and the heading gives a date of the seventh year of Hadrian, i.e., A.D. 124. Another Greek document is a certificate of debt, incomplete, but dated to the time of the emperor Commodus, A.D. 180–92. These and other Greek documents are all on papyrus, but some are on skin and give administrative registers, civil and military. Jewish names like Josephus, Jesus, Saulus, and Simon appear, followed by numbers and signs.

The key to the occupation of the caves during the Roman period appeared with the finding of some Hebrew letters written on papyrus and dated to the time of

> the deliverance of Israel by the ministry of Simon ben Kosebah, prince of Israel.

This could be no other than the ill-fated Second Jewish Revolt of

A.D. 132–5, and the person named its leader, known elsewhere as Simon ben Kochebah or Kozebah. Indeed, two of the letters were written by this person himself to the officer in charge of the Murabba'at post, a certain Joshua ben Galgola. Here is a translation of one of them (pl. 7):

> Simon ben Kosebah to Joshua ben Galgola and the men of thy company; greetings. I call heaven to bear witness against me: *if* any one of the Galileans whom you have protected (or, delivered) cause trou[ble], I shall put fetters on your feet as I did to Ben Aphlul
>
> Simon ben Kosebah (. . .).

Unfortunately one of the key words of the text is broken, and the exact interpretation of others is doubtful, so that no finality is claimed for the above rendering, which is largely based on the suggestions of Dr Frank Cross. Milik, who is editing the Semitic section of the Murabba'at cache would rather render the middle passage:

> *if* any of the Galileans who are with you are wronged, I shall put fetters . . .

In any case, 'the Galileans' are probably refugees, and the first rendering implies that they are regarded by the leader of the Revolt as a potential fifth column, whilst the second wishes to ensure that they are not wronged in the distribution of rations, which at this juncture must have been becoming very short. The main interest of the letters lies in the personality of their author and his name. The two names by which we had previously known him, Ben (or Bar) Kochebah and Ben Kozebah, mean respectively 'Son of the Star' and 'Son of the Lie', and were nicknames given him on the one hand by his supporters who regarded him as the Messiah, fulfilling the 'Star' prophecy of Numbers xxiv. 17, and on the other by his enemies who ridiculed his pretensions with this opprobrious title. Now that we see for the first time that his name was really *Kosebah*, the way in which both plays were easily possible can be understood. The 'heaven' of the opening call to witness is of course a surrogate for God, and Cross makes the interesting point that the call to heaven for witness is exactly paralleled by the words of St Paul in his second letter to the Corinthians, i. 23:

> But I call God for a witness upon my soul, that to spare you . . .

Another letter addressed to the officer in charge of the post came from Bēth Māshekô, a place presumably farther south and under Nabatean influence, to judge from the form of the name (pl. 39). This reads, according to Milik's rendering:

> From the administrators of Bēth Māshekô, from Joshua and from El'azar, to Joshua ben Galgola, chief of the camp; greetings. Let it be known to you that the heifer which Joseph ben Ariston bought from Jacob ben Judah, who resides in Bēth Māshekô, is his by purchase. Moreover, were it not that the Gentiles are so close to us I should have gone up and made a settlement (of all outstanding claims) with you on this, that you may not say that it was out of disrespect that I have not come up to you.
>
> Fare you and the whole house of Israel well.
>
> Joshua ben El'azar wrote it.
> El'azar ben Joseph wrote it.
> Jacob ben Judah, for himself.
> Saul ben El'azar, witness.
> Joseph bar Joseph, witness.
> Jacob bar Joseph, attestant.

'Were it not that the Gentiles are so close to us' tells its own pathetic story, as the Roman legions closed in on Bēth Māshekô, and it is unlikely that Joseph ben Ariston enjoyed the possession of his newly purchased heifer or indeed of anything else for very long after this letter was written.

The biblical texts from Murabba'at are, as has already been pointed out, of a strictly Massoretic character, indicating that by 132 the standardization of that tradition had most probably taken place. The most complete exemplar recovered from these caves is a scroll of the Minor Prophets which, although it has suffered considerably through damp, with a consequent blackening of the leather over large sections, on which only infra-red photography can show any writing at all, nevertheless is still recognizably a scroll. It was brought to Saad at the Museum in December of 1954, by Bedouin who said that, shortly before, one of their number had found a small cave on the opposite side of the Wady, and in exploring it had discovered a small rectangular hole in the side. He had reached up with his pick and dislodged the stone blocking the entrance, whereupon the scroll had fallen out. The price asked was £2,200, which was not exorbitant in view of the cost of the other Dead Sea material. However, the money was simply not there. The Jordan Government was asked again to help and eventually agreed to do so, but the delay in agreement, and then in payment, was such that considerable concern was felt among us for the fate of the remainder of the fragments from Qumran still known to be in Bedouin hands. Again we longed to have had a fund readily available for the immediate purchase of this priceless material as it became available.

Other, small, fragments found included parts of the books of Genesis, Exodus, Deuteronomy, and Isaiah, and these all came from a confined corner of the Second Cave, and bear the marks of purposeful destruction (pl. 40). In particular, the fragments of Genesis xxxii–xxxiv are found in a thin strip which has been torn violently across three columns of the scroll. Of a scroll of Isaiah we have only the beginning remaining, but there is one complete phylactery nearly seven inches long, written on a very fine skin whose width varies between half-an-inch and an inch. In a minute, semi-cursive hand, it has the three passages Exodus xiii. 1–10, 11–16, Deuteronomy xi. 13–21 in that order. A small separate piece has on it the Shema' of Deuteronomy vi. 4–9. These are the four biblical texts which the rabbis prescribe for phylacteries, and are particularly interesting in view of the 'unorthodox' phylacteries from Qumran, showing that in this as in the matter of the biblical texts themselves, the standardizing influence of the central authority had by this time made itself felt.

Another important aspect of the Murabba'at discoveries is the new and welcome light it has thrown upon the language and palaeography of second-century Judaism. It will have been noticed that the letters written to the military post at Murabba'at were written in Hebrew, as were some of the contracts. This hardly accords with the oft-expressed view that long before this Hebrew had become a dead language. One can understand a dead language surviving for purely religious purposes where a conservatism in this respect lends an air of sanctity to the ritual, but letters are usually written in the spoken language of the time, and there would similarly be little point in drawing up a contract in a language foreign to its participants. We must therefore suppose that Hebrew was still being used in the first half of the second century of our era among Jews of Palestine, in a live and forceful manner which gives no sign either of being at its last gasp or of artificial resurrection for political or nationalistic ends.

The history of the cursive script of Hebrew extending over the turn of the era has been almost entirely blank for want of first-hand material. Now, thanks to Qumran, we are well equipped for the period up to 70, and from Murabba'at up to 135, but it must be admitted that the cursive Hebrew from the latter cache was so strange to our eyes that it needed deciphering like any code. Many of the letters were completely unlike anything that had ever been seen before in Hebrew palaeography, and an example which Milik finally solved and showed to be a marriage contract is to be seen on pl. 41. Such documents are a tantalizing reminder of how little we know about the language and writing of this sparsely documented period of Judaism.

An Unknown Source

Another batch of manuscript material brought to the Museum by the Bedouin in the middle of July 1952 seems to have come from a part of the Dead Sea region which has still never been properly determined. They comprise some Nabatean and Jewish papyri of business and marriage contracts, and, most important, a fragmentary Greek text on leather of the Minor Prophets. The dating of these documents is not in doubt, since one of the contracts bears the date 'the third year of the Freedom of Israel', that is the last year of the Second Revolt, 135. This is how it runs, according to Milik's rendering:

> The twentieth of Iyyar, the third year of the Freedom of Israel, at Kephar-Bebayu; Hadar, son of Judah, of Kephar-Bebayu, has said to Eliazar, son of Eliazar, dwelling in the same place. I, of my own will, to-day have sold to you this day my house, which communicates on the north side with my court, so that you can make it communicate with your house. And you have no claim on me in the said court. I have sold (it) to you for a sum amounting to 8 denarii, the equivalent of 2 tetradrachmae, the total price. For all time Eliazar has rights in the buying of this house, stones, beams, *furniture,* all that there is . . . ground. The limits of this house (which you) Eliazar are buying: to the East *the property of Jonathan,* to the north the court, to the west and south the (ground) purchase. And you have no claim on me in my court, and I, Hadar, may not enter or go out from this day and for ever. And I am guarantor and surety for the sale of the said house from this day and for ever.
>
> And I, Salome, daughter of Simon, wife of the said Hadar, may raise no objections to the sale of the said house for ever more. And our present and future assets will serve you as guarantee.
>
> This document is 'plain', and *these* have signed herein:
>
> Hadar, son of Judah, a party, has written.
> Salome, daughter of Simon, a party has written.

Eliazar, son of Mattathiah . . .
Simon, son of Joseph, a witness.
Eliazar, son of Joseph, a witness.
Judah, son of Judah, a witness.

The place, Kephar-Bebayu, is not otherwise known (apart from a possible reference in the apocryphal book of Judith), but is probably to be located in the south of Palestine. The description of the document as 'plain' means that, unlike other papyrus contracts coming from the same source, it is not written twice on the same sheet. This convention, known otherwise from Egyptian papyri, allowed the top part, in the case of one of the marriage contracts written very small and hurriedly, to be sealed and kept in that condition until it became the subject of a legal dispute. Then the seals would be broken and only the top part taken into consideration for judging the dispute, in the case of wilful alteration of the lower copy. The signatures are on the back of the sheet, and carefully written *below* the top copy so that even when the 'original' is sealed, the names may still remain visible, presumably in case they have to be called to testify as witnesses. In actual fact, the lack of needle holes in the papyrus of the marriage contract referred to indicates that the double copying was merely a convention and that the sealing need not at this time be carried out. This particular contract, though badly broken, is interesting for a number of reasons, as Milik points out. It is dated to the seventh day of Adar (year missing), in Harôdônā', identical with the modern Khirbet Haredan, the hill near Cedron, a few miles from Jerusalem, possibly the home of two of David's heroes, Shammah and Elika, the *Harodites* (cp. 2 Samuel xxiii. 25). In the Talmud and Targums the place is mentioned as that from which the scapegoat was sent out into the desert, laden with the sins of the people, though comparison of this animal with the bridegroom is perhaps not kind. But in connexion with the scapegoat, it is interesting to note that in I Enoch it is probable that the Greek name for the site where the chief of demons is cast into the pit is to be amended to represent this place name.

The Greek text of the Minor Prophets referred to above as found in the same cache, will have a profound effect on future Septuagint studies. The beautiful uncial writing would point to a palaeographical date towards the end of the first century of our era, which would allow of the forty or fifty years' wear till the time of the Second Revolt, which the condition of the manuscript would support (pl. 42). The parts of the text surviving are from Micah,

Jonah, Nahum, Habakkuk, Zephaniah, and Zechariah, and these Father Barthélemy has subjected to a close scrutiny for their recensional correspondences. The results of his study are exciting and have particular reference to a work written in the second century by the great Christian apologist, Justin. This purports to be the dialogue of a controversy with the Jew Trypho, and Justin is complaining of the attitude of the Jews towards the venerable Greek tradition of the Septuagint, which they had abandoned since its adoption by the Christian Church, claiming that it was not a trustworthy basis for the claims of Christian dogmatics. This, says Justin, is unworthy of their ancestors, those seventy-two venerable scholars who performed the work of translation some four hundred years before. Furthermore, he complains that the rabbis were circulating Greek translations which were less dependable than the LXX, and goes on to give parallel examples from the old translation and the modern recensions to prove his point. It will be readily understood that, from the point of view of determining the original nature of the LXX text and how far it has been effected by later translations, Justin's book has always been of considerable interest to textual scholars. The trouble has been, however, that the earliest copy of the work extant goes back only to the fourteenth century and between then and its composition it could have suffered considerable modifications, particularly in the most important minutiae of the comparative renderings. Furthermore, the authenticity of the Dialogue itself is open to question, and even if perfectly reliable, the rabbinic Greek text Justin quotes may have been a purely local production, which could have had no effect on the general transmission of the LXX. Now, suddenly, out of the Judaean desert, this new Greek manuscript has put the matter in a new light. Barthélemy shows that the text of Justin's version agrees remarkably with this new manuscript at the hundreds of instances where comparison is possible. He shows further that this text is nothing more than a scholarly revision of the old LXX, bringing it closer to the Hebrew of the Massoretic text. In other words, Justin was perfectly correct in his arguments: the Church's Bible was not a christianizing recension specially developed by the Christian Community for dogmatic reasons, but the old Septuagint made centuries before and still being followed by the rabbinic scholars of his day. Furthermore, the rabbinic version of Aquila, long recognized as a more literal rendering of the Hebrew, and stemming from violently anti-Christian circles at the end of the first century, agrees twenty-eight times with our new text where it differs from the LXX, and shows that not only was this text also a mere revision of the LXX but that, furthermore, it was itself based on an earlier recension in the same tradition as the newly found fragments. Symmachus also, who gave a more free rendering of the Hebrew, unmarred by the pedantic literalness of Aquila, also seems to have been using our recension, for Barthélemy points out six places where, although Aquila's rendering is unknown to us, Symmachus goes with our text against the LXX. It can be shown that where he differs from our text it is simply in order to give a better Greek style.

It thus appears certain that our text enjoyed a considerable diffusion and authority in rabbinic circles of the first and second centuries. Even the Fifth Column of Origen's Hexapla, that scholar's own revision of the LXX text, seems to have been based on it, according to Barthélemy.

If this scholar is correct in his deductions, the overall effect is certainly to support the claim of the old LXX recension to a length of honourable lineage over the later, more local translations, and with the now proved fact from Qumran that it was itself a faithful rendering of a genuine Hebrew tradition, in at least the historical books, this new evidence should serve to increase still further our respect for the LXX as a reliable witness to a very early textual tradition.

Khirbet Mird

A somewhat less important, yet nevertheless interesting cache of documentary material was uncovered in July 1952 by the indefatigable Bedouin at Khirbet Mird, two and a half miles NE. of the Mar Saba, the ancient Christian monastery not far from Bethlehem. The Arabs had burrowed into the underground chamber of a ruined monastery there, and had produced a number of Greek and Arabic papyri as well as some Christo-Palestinian Syriac works. All the documents are, of course, very much later than those coming from Qumran or Murabba'at, and date not earlier than the beginning of the Byzantine period, say, at the earliest, the fifth century, and running on till the ninth, when the monastery was destroyed. Milik has published one of the Aramaic letters, dating it approximately to the seventh century. It runs thus:

> From Blessed-be-the-Lord and the Sinner, Gabriel; to the head of the Monastery of our Lords and fathers. I beg of you that prayers be offered for me on account of the tribe, on account of whom my heart trembles. Peace be unto you from the Father and from the Son and from the Holy Spirit. Amen.

Milik suggests that 'the tribe' are local Bedouin marauders.

Biblical documents include parts of the books of Joshua, Matthew, Luke, Acts, and the letter of Paul to the Colossians, the first two and the last being hitherto quite unknown in Christo-Palestinian Aramaic. Khirbet Mird was officially excavated between February and April 1953 by a Belgian expedition under the leadership of Professor R. De Langhe of Louvain. They confirmed the place of origin of the fragments and found more Greek and Arabic papyri and Aramaic fragments on their own account.

APPENDIX IV

THE COPPER SCROLL

As has already been said in Chapter Five, on the 14th March 1952, the party investigating the cliffs behind the monastery found a cave whose roof had collapsed in antiquity. Lying close up against an inner wall were two rolled up copper strips, and scattered nearby scores of leather scroll fragments and the remains of typical Qumran scroll jars. There could thus be no doubt that all these objects were connected with the Sect, but attempts to open the strips were frustrated by the extremely brittle nature of the oxydized metal, which simply crumbled to dust at any manipulation of the edges. This was most tantalizing since clearly visible on the outside of the rolls were Aramaic or Hebrew letters, heavily indented from the inside. Only a few words could be read through the incrustation of the copper oxide, and it was at least plain that this was no biblical document. Very gently, the strips were lifted, coated with paraffin wax, and taken to the Palestine Archaeological Museum. There they rested for three years, awaiting a solution to the problem of opening them without damaging the inscription. Reports on the chemical composition and state of the metal were sought from various quarters, and in the Johns Hopkins University of Baltimore considerable progress was made on the general problem of reconstituting corroded metals with particular reference to this matter, under the direction of Dr Corwin of that institution. These results have already proved of real worth in the archaeological field, but as far as the present problem was concerned, it was clear that the metal had completely corroded, and the chances of restoring the copper's flexibility were nil. The obvious solution was to cut the rolls into strips, thus revealing the inner surface, and provided this could be done without disintegration of the material, no harm would come to the inscription itself. There was clearly nothing of artistic value in the strips themselves, so the sacrifice of their original form could well be afforded.

In the spring of 1955, while on a visit to Jordan, I suggested to Harding that if his government were willing to let the strips out of the country, I felt sure that in Manchester I could find a responsible concern able and willing to undertake this delicate task, and which would, at the same time, be sufficiently accessible for me to follow the progress of the work and advise on the cutting lines. In the following May, Harding wrote asking me to follow the suggestion further my end. After one or two unsuccessful inquiries, I contacted Dr B. V. Bowden, principal of the Manchester College of Technology, who received the project with real enthusiasm, promising every facility of this splendid institution for the solution of our problem. That very afternoon, he asked a member of his staff, Professor H. Wright Baker, of the department of Engineering, to take the matter in hand, and make his suggestions. I made my report to Jordan, and the matter was placed before the government of that country. As a result, Harding was able to bring the smaller of the strips to Britain in the following summer, and on 13th July handed it over to the care of Dr Bowden.

The preparation of a suitable cutting machine began immediately, and by the time I had returned from my summer visit to Jordan, work on the strip itself was ready to begin. The roll had been pierced through the centre with an aluminium spindle, itself firmly mounted on a small trolley, which could be made to move forward on rails directly under the spring-loaded arm carrying the saw. This was of 2 in. diameter, and of .006 in. thickness, and being completely controllable by the operator could thus be made to cut lengthwise along the roll to the exact depth required to penetrate one 'leaf' at a time. There still remained the problem of preventing the material from shattering under the saw, and this was eventually overcome by coating the outside with 'Araldite' plastic, and baking the whole roll in a moderate temperature for a couple of hours. This gave the strip concerned a tenacious skin which prevented shattering, even though some clean breaks were unavoidable in lifting strips adhering inside. These breaks were easily repaired, however, and did not mar the inscription.

On the side of the roll opposite the outer edge there was a most fortunately placed column margin, so that there could be no difficulty about the position of the first cut, which was made on the evening of Friday, 30th September 1955. I went to the college as soon as possible the next morning, and began cleaning the freshly removed strip. The dust from the cave was several millimetres thick but to our great joy, most of it fell away quite easily, and indeed, inner adhesions were mercifully few. Mounted on the table bearing the cutting machine was a dental drill, which, together with the small nylon brushes which could be fitted to the instrument, made the work of cleaning and removing adhesions comparatively simple. Thus the face of the first strip was cleaned, and the writing which had lain hidden for nigh on two thousand years once more faced the light of day. As word after word became plain, and the import of the whole document inescapable, I could hardly believe my eyes. Indeed, I resolutely refused to credit the obvious until more strips had been removed and cleaned. However, after another column or two of the script had been deciphered, I rushed air letters to Harding with the news. At least I could now feel my excitement was being shared with another, although it was immediately obvious that the strictest secrecy would have to be kept on the matter for some little time.

Now the coating, baking, cutting, and cleaning developed into a comparatively easy routine, and two or even three cuts a day became possible. The most tricky part of the process was deciding where to make the next cut so as to avoid going through letters visible from the outside. Where this was impossible, we had to arrange to make the cut only across diagonal or horizontal strokes, since to go along a vertical engraving would completely obliterate the stroke. Happily this only happened rarely, where the indentation on the outside was not clear enough to give an exact indication of the line made by the stylus.

Four columns of writing appeared in that part of the scroll, for such it turned out to be. Clearly it had been made as a replica of a normal leather scroll, except that instead of stitching, the three copper 'skins' had been riveted at the edges, and in the final rolling, the scroll had broken across at one of the rivet lines. Instead of the quill, the scribe had used a stylus with a point perhaps an eighth of an inch wide, although it was also clear that he had been unpractised in his new art. The writing began with quite large letters, but towards the bottom of a page they would become smaller and more cramped. He had made some errors, many undoubtedly deliberate to confuse the unauthorized reader. This device certainly often succeeded, and I could not help feeling something of an intruder as I wrestled with this painstaking document, which had held its secret so well since the day a frightened priest had thrown it in the cave, as he escaped from the smoking ruins of the monastery.

Soon this part of the scroll was opened, and we impatiently awaited the arrival of the larger portion, which, in fact, contained the beginning of the scroll. I was especially anxious to see this since I hoped it might contain a title to the document, with a proper name or geographical location. Although I was not to be entirely disappointed in this, it was many weeks before the second roll arrived in Britain. The complete transcription of the first part, together with a provisional translation and notes, I had despatched to Harding in Amman on 26th November, but it was not until the very end of the year that permission was finally granted for the second part to leave the country. It actually arrived in Manchester on the 2nd January, and the first cut was made on the 11th. In five days all the eight columns of this portion lay open, making a total of twelve for the complete document, which had an unrolled length of some eight feet. The first line, buried deep in the centre of the second roll, gave up its secret at 9 p.m. on 16th January 1956. That night I sent Harding a cable, telling him it was open, and adding a biblical reference which I hoped would convey the message of the first line.

My readings followed by air, and the complete scroll was packed and returned to Jordan in April 1956. The news of the opening had been released before this, and now the world knows that in the main the hypothesis of Professor K. G. Kuhn, formed long ago on the basis of a few words visible from the outside, has been proved marvellously accurate. It is indeed an inventory of the Sect's most treasured possessions, buried in various locations. Further information must wait on the release and publication of the whole text, a task entrusted by Father De Vaux, as head of the expedition which found the cave, to Father Joseph Milik of the French School in Jerusalem.

BIBLIOGRAPHY

The following represents a *selection* of the more recent publications on the Scrolls. For a very full bibliography up to 1952, the reader is referred to Professor H. H. Rowley's book, *The Zadokite Fragments and the Dead Sea Scrolls* of that date.

ABBREVIATIONS

AfO	*Archiv für Orientforschung*
AThR	*Anglican Theological Review*
BA	*Biblical Archaeologist*
BASOR	*Bulletin of the American Schools of Oriental Research*
BIES	*Bulletin of the Israel Exploration Society*
BJRL	*Bulletin of the John Rylands Library*
CBQ	*Catholic Biblical Quarterly*
EphThLov	*Ephemerides Theologicae Lovanienses*
ET	*Expository Times*
HTR	*Harvard Theological Review*
HUCA	*Hebrew Union College Annual*
IEJ	*Israel Exploration Journal*
JBL	*Journal of Biblical Literature*
JJS	*Journal of Jewish Studies*
JQR	*Jewish Quarterly Review*
JTS	*Journal of Theological Studies*
JNES	*Journal of Near Eastern Studies*
NRTh	*Nouvelle Revue Théologique*
PEQ	*Palestine Exploration Quarterly*
RB	*Revue Biblique*
RHPR	*Revue d'Histoire et de Philosophie Religieuses*
RHR	*Revue de l'Histoire des Religions*
ThLZ	*Theologische Literaturzeitung*
ThZ	*Theologische Zeitschrift*
VT	*Vetus Testamentum*
ZAW	*Zeitschrift für die alttestamentliche Wissenschaft*
ZNW	*Zeitschrift für die neutestamentliche Wissenschaft*
ZTK	*Zeitschrift für Theologie und Kirche*
ZRGg	*Zeitschrift für Religions und Geistesgeschichte*

S. Abramson and H. L. Ginsberg, 'On the Aramaic Deed of Sale of the Third Year of the Second Jewish Revolt', BASOR 136, Dec. 1954, p. 17 ff.

W. F. Albright, 'New Light on Early Recensions of the Hebrew Bible', BASOR 140, Dec. 1955, pp. 27–33.

J. M. ALLEGRO, 'A Newly Discovered Fragment of a Commentary on Psalm 37 from Qumrân', PEQ 86, 1954, pp. 69–75.

J. R. AUDET, 'Affinités littéraires et doctrinales du Manuel de Discipline', RB 60, 1953, pp. 41–82.

M. BAILLET, 'Fragments araméens de Qumrân 2. Description de la Jérusalem Nouvelle', RB 62, 1955, pp. 222–45.

H. BARDTKE, *Die Handschriftenfunde am Toten Meer,* 1952.

'Die Parascheneinteilung der Jesajarolle I vom Qumrân', *Festschrift Franz Dornseiff zum 65. Geburtstag,* ed. H. KUSCH, 1953, pp. 33–75.

'Bemerkungen zu den beiden Texten aus dem Bar Kochba-Aufstand', ThLZ 79, 1954, cols. 295–304.

'Die Kriegsrolle von Qumran übersetzt', ThLZ 80, 1955, cols. 401–20.

D. BARTHÉLEMY, 'Redécouverte d'un chaînon manquant de l'histoire de la Septante', RB 60, 1953, pp. 18–29.

D. BARTHÉLEMY and J. T. MILIK, *Discoveries in the Judaean Desert I: Qumran, Cave 1,* 1955.

F. BAUMGÄRTEL, 'Zur Liturgie in der "Sektenrolle" vom Toten Meer', ZAW 64, 1953, pp. 263 ff.

J. M. BAUMGARTEN, 'Sacrifice and Worship among the Jewish Sectarians of the Dead Sea (Qumrân) Scrolls', HTR 46, 1953, pp. 141–59.

J. M. BAUMGARTEN and M. MANSOOR, 'Studies in the New *HODAYOT* (Thanksgiving Hymns)', JBL 74, 1955, pp. 115–24, 188–95.

W. BAUMGARTNER, 'Wiederum die palästinischen Handschriftenfunde', ThZ 9, 1953, pp. 469–73.

W. BAUMGARTNER, 'Neue Handschriftenfunde am Toten Meer', AfO 16, 1954, pp. 379–82.

'Die Bedeutung der Höhlenfunde aus Palästina für die Theologie', *Schweizerische Theologische Umschau* 24, 1954, pp. 49–63.

Neue Funde und Grabungen am Toten Meer, AfO 17, 1955, pp. 213–15.

D. M. BEEGLE, 'Ligatures with Waw and Yodh in the D.S. Isaiah Scroll', BASOR 129, Feb. 1953, pp. 11–14.

G. BERARDI and P. BOCCACCIO, *Interpretatio Habacuc* (*DSH*), 1955.

H. BIRKELAND, 'Some Linguistic Remarks on the Dead Sea Scrolls', *Norse Teologisk Tidsskrift* 56, 1955, pp. 24–35.

S. A. BIRNBAUM, 'The Date of the Hymns Scroll', PEQ, 1952, pp. 94–103.
The Qumrân (Dead Sea) Scrolls and Palaeography (BASOR Suppl. St. Nos. 13–14), 1952.
'Bar Kokhba and Akiba', PEQ 86, 1954, pp. 23–32.
M. BLACK, 'Theological Conceptions in the DSS', *Svensk Exegetisk Årsbok* 18–19, 1953–54, pp. 72–97.
P. BOCCACCIO, see G. BERARDI.
P. A. H. DE BOER, 'Étude sur le sens de la Racine QWH' *Oudtestamentische Studien* 10, 1954, pp. 225–46.
F. M. BRAUN, 'L'arrière-fond judaique du quatrième évangile et la communauté de l'Alliance', RB 62, 1955, pp. 5–44.
H. BRAUN, '"Umkehr" in Spätjüdisch-häretischer und in frühchristlicher Sicht', ZTK 1, 1953, pp. 243–58.
'Beobachtungen zur Tora-Verschärfung im häretischen Spätjudentum (Manual of Discipline und Damaskusschrift)', ZNW 45, 1954, pp. 134 ff.
J. R. BROWN, 'Pesher in the Habakkuk Scroll', ET 66, 1955, p. 125.
R. E. BROWN, 'The Qumran Scrolls and the Johannine Gospel and Epistles', CBQ 17, 1955, pp. 403–19, 559–74.
W. H. BROWNLEE, 'The Manuscripts of Isaiah from which DSIa was copied', BASOR 127, Oct. 1952, pp. 16–21.
'The Servant of the Lord in the Qumran Scrolls', BASOR 132, Dec. 1953, pp. 8–15; 135, Oct. 1954, pp. 33–38.
W. H. BROWNLEE and J. REIDER, 'On MSḤTY in the Qumran Scrolls', BASOR 134, 1954, p. 27 f.
W. H. BROWNLEE, 'Emendations of the Dead Sea Manual of Discipline and some notes concerning the Habakkuk Midrash', JQR 45, 1954, pp. 141–58; 198–218.
'John the Baptist in the New Light of Ancient Scrolls', *Interpretation,* 9, 1955, pp. 71–90.
M. BURROWS, 'The Messiahs of Aaron and Israel', AThR 34, 1952, pp. 202–6.
The Dead Sea Scrolls, 1955.
J. V. CHAMBERLAIN, 'Another Qumrân Thanksgiving Psalm', JNES 14, 1955, pp. 32–41.
'Further Elucidation of a Messianic Thanksgiving Psalm from Qumrân', JNES 1955, pp. 181 f.
J. CARMIGNAC, 'Les Kittim dans la "Guerre des fils de lumière contre les fils de ténèbres"', NRTh 87, 1955, pp. 737–48.
J. COPPENS, *Les documents du désert de Juda et les origines du*

Christianisme (*Analecta Lovaniensa Biblica et Orientalia* 39), 1953.
'La Secte de Qumran et son attente eschatologique', *La Nouvelle Clio* 5, 1953, pp. 5–9.
'Nieuwe Psalmen van Qumran', *Wetenschappeljke Tijdingen* 15, 1955, cols. 156–58.

B. COUROYER, 'A propos des dépôts de manuscrits dans des jarres', RB 70, 1955, pp. 76–81.

F. M. CROSS, Jnr., 'A New Qumrân Biblical Fragment related to the original Hebrew underlying the Septuagint', BASOR 132, Dec. 1953, pp. 15–26.
'The Manuscripts of the Dead Sea Caves', BA 17, 1954, pp. 2–21.
'The Scrolls from the Judaean Wilderness', *The Christian Century*, 3 August, 1955, pp. 889 ff.
'The Scrolls and the Old Testament', *ibid.*, 10 August, 1955, pp. 920 ff.
'The Essenes and their Master', *ibid.*, 17 August, 1955, pp. 944 ff.
'The Scrolls and the New Testament', *ibid.*, 24 August, 1955, pp. 968 ff.
'The Oldest Manuscripts from Qumran', JBL 74, 1955, pp. 147–72.

O. CULLMAN, 'Die neuentdeckten Qumrantexte und das Judenchristentum der Pseudoklementinen', *Neutestamentliche Studien für R. Bultmann* (ZNW 21), pp. 35–51.
'The Significance of the Qumran Texts for Research into the Beginnings of Christianity', JBL 74, 1955, pp. 213–26.

J. DANIÉLOU, 'La Communauté de Qumrân et l'organization de l'Église ancienne', RHPR 35, 1955, pp. 104–15.

W. D. DAVIES, '"Knowledge" in the Dead Sea Scrolls and Matthew 11: 25–30', HThR 46, 1953, pp. 113–39.

M. DELCOR, 'Le sacerdoce les lieux de culte les rites et les fêtes dans les documents de Khirbet Qumrân', RHR 1953, pp. 5–41.
'Contribution à l'étude de la législation des sectaires de Damas et de Qumrân', RB 61, 1954, pp. 533–53; 62, 1955, pp. 60–75.
'Des diverses manières d'écrire le Tétragramme sacré dans les anciens documents hébraiques', RHR, 147, 1955, pp. 145–73.
'La Guerre des fils de lumière contre les fils de ténèbres en le Manuel du parfait combattant (Traduction Annotée), NRTh 87, 1955, pp. 3–30.

C. DETAYE, 'Le Cadre historique de midrash d'Habacuc', EphThLov 30, 1954, pp. 323–43.

A. DUPONT-SOMMER, 'La sainteté du Signe "noun" dans le Manuel de Discipline', *Bulletins de la Classe des Lettres et des Sciences Morales et Politiques de l'Académie Royale de Belgique,* 38, 1952, pp. 184–93.

'L'Instruction sur les deux Esprits dans le "Manuel de Discipline"', RHR 142, 1952, pp. 5–35.

The Jewish Sect of Qumrân and the Essenes (tr. R. D. BARNETT), 1954.

'Le problème des influences étrangères sur la secte juive de Qumrân', RHPR 35, 1955, pp. 75–92.

'La mère du Messie et la mère de l'Aspic dans un Hymne de Qumrân', RHR, 147, 1955, pp. 174–88.

'"Règlement de la guerre des fils de lumière": traduction et notes', RHR 148, 1955, pp. 25–43.

'Quelques remarques sur le Commentaire d'Habacuc, à propos d'un livre récent', VT 5, 1955, pp. 113–29.

'Le Chef des rois de Yāwān dans l'ÉCRIT DE DAMAS', *Semitica* 5, 1955, pp. 41–57.

R. DUSSAUD, 'Khirbet Qumran', *Syria* 32, 1955, pp. 161–3.

K. ELLIGER, *Studien zum Habakuk-Kommentar vom Toten Meer,* 1953.

W. R. FARMER, 'The Economic Basis of the Qumran Community', *Theologische Zeitschrift* 11, 1955, pp. 295–308.

J. G. FÉVRIER, 'La Date des Textes de 'Ayin Fashkha en Écriture Paléo-Hebraique', *Journal Asiatique* 239, 1951, pp. 275–82.

J. A. FITZMYER, 'The Qumran Scrolls, the Ebionites and their literature', *Theological Studies* 16, 1955, pp. 335–72.

D. FLUSSER, 'The Connection between the Apocryphal *Ascensio Isaiae* and the Dead Sea Scrolls', BIES 17, 1952, pp. 28–46.

'The Apocryphal Book of *Ascensio Isaiae* and the Dead Sea Sect', IEJ 3, 1953, pp. 30–47.

C. T. FRITSCH, 'Herod the Great and the Qumran Community', JBL 74, 1955, pp. 173–81.

B. GÄRTNER, 'The Habakkuk Commentary (DSH) and the Gospel of St Matthew', *Studia Theologica* 8, 1954, pp. 1–24.

H. L. GINSBERG, 'Notes on the Two Published Letters to Jeshua Ben Galgolah', BASOR 131, Oct. 1953, pp. 25–27. See S. ABRAMSON.

G. S. GLANZMAN, 'Sectarian Psalms from the Dead Sea', *Theological Studies* 13, 1952, pp. 487–524.

R. GOOSSENS, 'Les Kittim du Commentaire d'Habacuc', *La Nouvelle Clio* 4, 1952, pp. 137–70.
'Le Vocabulaire du Manuel de Discipline', *La Nouvelle Clio,* 4, 1952, pp. 297 ff.
'L'énigme du signe "nun" dans le Manuel de Discipline', *La Nouvelle Clio* 6, 1954, pp. 5–39.
M. H. GOTTSTEIN, 'Bemerkungen zu Eissfeldt's "Variae Lectiones der Jesaia-Rolle"', *Biblica* 34, 1953, pp. 212–21.
'Studies in the Language of the Dead Sea Scrolls', JJS 4, 1953, pp. 104–7.
'Bible Quotations in the Sectarian Dead Sea Scrolls', VT 3, 1953, pp. 79–82.
'A DSS Biblical Variant in a Medieval Treatise', VT 3, 1953, pp. 187 ff.
'Die Jesaia-Rolle im Lichte von Peschitta und Targum', *Biblica* 35, 1954, pp. 51–71.
'Die Jesaia-Rolle und das Problem der hebräischen Bibelhandschriften', *Biblica* 35, 1954, pp. 429–42.
'Anti-Essene traits in the Dead Sea Scrolls', VT 4, 1954, pp. 141–7.
E. HAMMERSHAIMB, 'Handskriftfundene fra egnene ved Det døde hav', *Dansk Teologisk Tidsskrift* 1954, pp. 65–79.
G. L. HARDING, 'Khirbet Qumran and Wady Murabba'at', PEQ, 1952, pp. 104–9.
G. L. HARDING and W. L. REED, 'Archeological News from Jordan', BA 16, 1953, pp. 2–17.
A. J. B. HIGGINS, 'Priest and Messiah', VT 3, 1953, pp. 321–36.
A. M. HONEYMAN, 'Notes on a Teacher and a Book', JJS 4, 1953, pp. 131–2.
A. JAUBERT, 'Le calendrier des Jubilées et de la Secte de Qumrân: ses origines bibliques', VT 3, 1953, pp. 250–64.
'La Date de la dernière Cène', RHR 1954, pp. 140–73.
S. E. JOHNSON, 'The Dead Sea Manual of Discipline and the Jerusalem Church of Acts', ZAW 66, 1954, pp. 106–20.
'Paul and the Manual of Discipline', HTR 48, 1955, pp. 157–65.
J. A. JUNGMANN, 'Altchristliche Gebetsordnung im Lichte des Regelbuches von En Feschka', *Zeitschrift für Katholische Theologie,* 75, 1953, pp. 215–19.
P. KAHLE, 'The Karaites and the Manuscripts from the Cave', VT 3, 1953, pp. 82–4.

'Die im August 1952 entdeckte Lederrolle mit dem griechischen Text der kleinen Propheten und das Problem der Septuaginta', ThLZ 2, 1954, cols. 81–94.

J. L. KELSO, 'The Archeology of Qumran', JBL 74, 1955, pp. 141–6.

K. G. KUHN, '"Peirasmos, hamartia, sarx" im Neuen Testament und die damit zusammenhängenden Vorstellungen', ZTK, 1952, pp. 200–22.

'Die Sektenschrift und die Iranische Religion', ZTK, 1952, pp. 296–316.

'Les Rouleaux de cuivre de Qumrân', RB 61, 1954, pp. 193–205.

'Die beiden Messias Aarons und Israels', *New Testament Studies* 1, 1955, pp. 168–79.

F. A. W. VAN'T LAND and A. S. VAN DER WOUDE, 'De Habakukrol van "Ain Feschka"', *Vox Theologica*, Nov. 1952, pp. 41–49.

O. H. LEHMANN and S. M. STERN, 'A Legal Certificate from Bar Kochba's days', VT 3, 1953, pp. 391–6.

S. LOEWINGER, 'New Corrections to the Variae Lectiones of O. Eissfeldt', VT 4, 1954, pp. 80–87.

'The variants of DSI II', VT 4, 1954, pp. 155–63.

O. LÖFGREN, 'Zur Charakteristik des "vormasoretischen" Jesajatextes', *Donum Natalicium H. S. NYBERG oblatum*, 1955, pp. 171–84.

M. MANSOOR, see J. BAUMGARTEN.

R. MARCUS, 'Pharisees, Essenes and Gnostics', JBL 73, 1954, pp. 157–61.

'Philo, Josephus and the Dead Sea *Yaḥad*', JBL 71, 1952, pp. 207–9.

'Textual Notes on the Dead Sea Manual of Discipline', JNES 11, 1952, pp. 205–11.

W. J. MARTIN, *The Dead Sea Scroll of Isaiah*, 1954.

H. E. DEL MEDICO, 'La Traduction d'un texte démarqué dans le Manuel de Discipline (DSD x 1–9)', VT 6, 1956, pp. 34–39.

A. METZINGER, 'Die Handschriftenfunde am Toten Meer und das Neue Testament', *Biblica*, 36, 1955, pp. 457–81.

H. MICHAUD, 'Un mythe zervanite dans un des manuscrits de Qumran', VT 5, 1955, pp. 137–47.

'A propos du nom de Qumrân', RHPR 35, 1955, pp. 68–73.

A. MICHEL, *Le Maitre de Justice*, 1954.

J. T. MILIK, 'Fragments d'un Midrash de Michél dans les manuscrits de Qumrân', RB 59, 1952, pp. 412–8.

'Ein alter Bericht über den Fund hebräischer Handschriften in einer Höhle', *Archiv Orientální* 21, 1953, pp. 263–9.

'Une lettre de Siméon Bar Kokheba', RB 60, 1953, pp. 276–94.

'Une inscription et une lettre en araméen christopalestinien', RB 60, 1953, pp. 526–39.

'Un contrat juif de l'an 134 après Jésus-Christ' RB 61, 1954, pp. 182–90.

'Note additionelle sur le contrat juif de l'an 134 après Jésus-Christ', RB 62, 1955, pp. 253–4.

see D. BARTHÉLEMY.

G. MOLIN, 'Der Habakukkommentar von 'En Fešha in der alttestamentlichen Wissenschaft', ThZ, 8, 1952, pp. 340–57.

'Hat die Sekte von Qumrân Beziehungen zu Ägypten?' ThLZ 78, 1953, cols. 653–6.

Die Söhne des Lichtes, 1954.

S. MOSCATI, *I Manuscritti Ebraici del Deserto di Giuda,* 1955.

L. MOWRY, 'The Dead Sea Scrolls and the background for the Gospel of John', BA 17, 1954, pp. 78–97.

J. MUILENBERG, 'A Qoheleth Scroll from Qumrân', BASOR 135, Oct. 1954, pp. 20–28.

'Fragments of another Qumrân Isaiah Scroll', BASOR 135, Oct. 1954, pp. 28–32.

W. NAUCK, 'Lex insculpta (*ḥwq ḥrwt*) in der Sektenschrift', ZNW 46, 1955, pp. 138–140.

R. NORTH, 'Manuale Disciplinae et Liber Sapientiae', *Biblica* 35, 1954, p. 138.

'Qumran and its Archeology', CBQ 16, 1954, pp. 426–37.

'Qumran's own "Documentary Theory"', CBQ 17, 1955, pp. 25 f.

'The Qumran "Sadducees"', CBQ 17, 1955, pp. 158–63.

'The Damascus of Qumrân Geography', PEQ 1955, pp. 1–14, 34–48.

F. NÖTSCHER, '"Gesetz der Freiheit" in NT und in der, Mönchsgemeinde am Toten Meer', *Biblica* 34, 1953, pp. 193 f.

H. M. ORLINSKY, 'Studies in the St. Mark's Isaiah Scroll, IV', JQR 43, 1953, pp. 329–40.

–, V. IEJ, 4, 1954, pp. 5–8.

–, VI, HUCA 25, 1954, pp. 85–92.

–, VII, *Tarbiz* 24, 1954, pp. 4–8.

B. OTZEN, 'Die neugefundenen hebräischen Sektenschriften und die Testamente der zwölf Patriarchen', *Studia Theologica* 7 1954, pp. 125–57.

A. PARROT, 'Les manuscrits de la Mer Morte. Le point de vue archéologique', RHPR 35, 1955, pp. 61–65.

O. PLÖGER, 'Prophetistisches Erbe in den Sekten des frühen Judentums' ThLZ 79, 1954, cols. 291–6.

C. RABIN, 'The "Teacher of Righteousness" in the "Testaments of the Twelve Patriarchs"?' JJS 3, 1952, pp. 127 f.

The Zadokite Documents, 1954.

'Notes on the Habakkuk Scroll and the Zadokite Documents', VT 5, 1955, pp. 148–62.

'The Dead Sea Scrolls and the History of the Old Testament Text', JJS 6, 1955, pp. 174–82.

I. RABINOWITZ, 'A Hebrew Letter of the Second Century from Beth Mashko', BASOR, 131, Oct. 1953, pp. 21–24.

'Sequence and Dates of the Extra Biblical Dead Sea Scroll Texts and "Damascus Fragments"', VT 3, 1953, pp. 175–85.

'A reconsideration of "Damascus" and "390 years" in the Damascus (Zadokite) Fragments', JBL 73, 1954, pp. 11–53.

'Some notes on an Aramaic Contract from the Dead Sea Region', BASOR 136, Dec. 1954, pp. 15 f.

J. J. RABINOWITZ, 'Note sur la lettre de Bar Kokheba', RB 61, 1954, pp. 191 f.

'The Legal Document from Murabba'at', *Biblica,* 35, 1954, pp. 198–206.

'A clue to the Nabatean Contract from the Dead Sea Region', BASOR 139, Oct. 1955, pp. 11–14.

W. L. REED, 'The Qumrân Caves expedition of March 1952', BASOR 135, Oct. 1954, pp. 8–13.

see G. L. HARDING.

B. REICKE, 'Traces of Gnosticism in the Dead Sea Scrolls?' *New Testament Studies* 1, 1954, pp. 137–41.

'Die Verfassung der Urgemeinde im Lichte jüdischer Dokumente', ThZ 20, 1954, pp. 95–112.

J. REIDER, see W. H. BROWNLEE.

B. J. ROBERTS, 'The Dead Sea Scrolls and Apocalyptic Literature', *Oxford Society of Historical Theology Abstract of Proceedings for the Academic Year* 1952-3, pp. 29–35.

'The DSS and the Old Testament Scriptures', BJRL 36, 1953–4, pp. 75–96.

L. Rost, 'Das Verhältnis von "Damaskusschrift" und "Sektenrolle"', ThLZ 77, 1952, cols. 723–6.

'Der "Lehrer der Einung" und der "Lehrer der Gerechtigkeit"', ThLZ 78, 1955, cols. 143–8.

'Zum "Buch der Kriege der Söhne des Lichts gegen die Söhne der Finsternis"', ThLZ 80, 1955, cols. 205–8.

A. Rubinstein, 'Urban Halakah and Camp Rules in the "Cairo Fragments" of a Damascene Covenant', *Sefarad,* 1952, pp. 283–96.

'Notes on the use of the Tenses and the Variant Readings of the Isaiah Scroll', VT 3, 1953, pp. 92–95.

'Isaiah LII iv – MŠḤT – and the DSIa Variant', *Biblica* 35, 1954, pp. 475–9.

'Formal Agreement of Parallel Clauses in the Isaiah Scroll', VT 4, 1954, pp. 316–21.

'Singularities in the consecutive-tense constructions in the Isaiah Scroll', VT 5, 1955, pp. 180–8.

'The Appellation "Galileans" in Ben Kosebha's Letter to Ben Galgola', JJS 6, 1955, pp. 26–34.

'Conditional constructions in the Isaiah Scroll (DSIa), VT 6, 1956, pp. 69–79.

H. J. Schoeps, 'Ebionite Christianity', JTS 4, 1953, pp. 219–24.

'Das gnostische Judentum in den Dead Sea Scrolls', ZRGg 6, 1954, pp. 1–4, 276–9.

K. Schubert, 'Der Sektenkanon von En Feschcha und die Anfänge der jüdischen Gnosis', ThLZ 78, 1953, cols. 495–506.

R. B. Y. Scott, *Treasure from Judean Caves; The Story of the Dead Sea Scrolls,* 1955.

M. H. Segal, 'The Promulgation of the authoritative text of the Hebrew Bible', JBL 72, 195[illegible], pp. 35–47.

S. Segert, 'Ein alter Bericht über den Fund hebräischer Handschriften in einer Höhle', *Archiv Orientální* 21, 1953, pp. 263–9.

'Zur Habakuk-Rolle aus dem Funde vom Toten Meer', *Archiv Orientální* 21, 1953, pp. 218–39; 22, 1954, pp. 99–113, 444–59; 23, 1955, pp. 178–83, 364–73, 575–619.

L. H. Silberman, '"The Two Messiahs" of the Manual of Discipline', VT 5, 1955, pp. 77–82.

P. W. Skehan, 'A fragment of the "Song of Moses" (Deut. 32) from Qumrân', BASOR 136, Dec. 1954, pp. 12–15.

'The Text of Isaias at Qumrân', CBQ 17, 1955, pp. 158–63.

'Exodus in the Samaritan Recension from Qumrân', JBL 74, 1955, pp. 182–7.

M. Smith, 'Matthew 5:43: Hate Thine Enemy', HTR 45, 1952, pp. 71 ff.

H. F. D. Sparks, 'The Books of the Qumran Community', JTS 6, 1955, pp. 226–9.

J. Starcky, 'Un Contrat nabateen sur papyrus', RB 61, 1954, pp. 161–81.

E. Stauffer, 'Das "Gesetz der Freiheit" in der Ordensregel von Jericho', ThLZ 77, 1952, cols. 527–32.

K. Stendahl, *The School of St Matthew*, 1954.

S. M. Stern, see O. H. Lehmann.

E. L. Sukenik, *'Ôṣar ham-Megillôth hag-Genûzôth she-bîdhê ha-Ûnîbhersîṭāh ha-'Ibhrîth*, 1954.

S. Szyszman, 'A propos du Karaïsme et des textes de la Mer Morte', VT 2, 1952, pp. 343–48.

'Sur la geniza de Caire', VT 3, 1953, pp. 411 f.

S. Talmon, 'The Sectarian *YḤD* – a biblical Noun', VT 3, 1953, pp. 133–40.

J. L. Teicher, 'The Teaching of the pre-Pauline Church in the Dead Sea Scrolls, JJS 3, 1952, pp. 111–8; 139–50; 4, 1953, pp. 1–13; 49–58; 93–103; 139–53.

'Puzzling passages in the Damascus Fragments', JJS 5, 1954, pp. 139–47.

'Priests and Sacrifices in the Dead Scrolls', JJS 5, 1954, pp. 93–99.

J. C. Trever, 'Studies in the Problem of Dating the Dead Sea Scrolls', *Proceedings of the American Philosophical Society* 97, 1953, pp. 184–93.

R. De Vaux, 'Fouille au Khirbet Qumran', RB 60, 1953, pp. 83–106.

'Les grottes de Murabba'at et leurs documents', RB 60, 1953, pp. 245–67.

'Quelques textes hébreux de Murabba'at', RB 60, 1953, pp. 268–75.

'Exploration de la région de Qumrân', RB 60, 1953, pp. 504–61.

'Fouilles au Khirbet Qumrân', RB 61, 1954, pp. 206–36.

'Manuscrits du Désert de Juda', RB 61, 1954, pp. 630–3.

G. Vermès, *Les Manuscrits du Désert de Juda*, 1953.

'Le Cadre historique des manuscrits de la Mer Morte', *Recherches de Science religieuse*, 41, 1953, pp. 5–29, 203–30.

'A propos des Commentaires bibliques découverts à Qumrân', RHPR 35, 1955, pp. 95–102.

'Quelques Traditions de la Communauté de Qumrân', *Cahiers Sioniens*, 1955, pp. 25–58.

A. VINCENT, *Les Manuscrits hébreux du désert de Juda* (Libraire Arthème Fayard), 1955.

E. VOGT, 'Textus praemasoreticus ex Qumran', *Biblica* 35, 1954, pp. 263–6.

M. WALLENSTEIN, 'Some lexical material in the Judean Scrolls', VT 4, 1954, pp. 211–4.

'A Hymn from the Scrolls', VT 5, 1955, pp. 277–83.

'A Striking Hymn from the Dead Sea Scrolls', BJRL 38, 1955, pp. 241–65.

P. WERNBERG-MØLLER, 'Observations on the Interchange of '*Ayin* and *Ḥeth* in the Manual of Discipline', VT 3, 1953, pp. 104–7.

'Notes on the Manual of Discipline (DSD) I 18, II 9, III 1–4, 9, VII 10–12, and XI 21–23', VT 3, 1953, pp. 195–202.

'*ṢDQ, ṢDYQ, ṢDWQ* in the Zadokite Fragments (CDC), in the Manual of Discipline (DSD) and the Habakkuk Commentary (DSH)', VT 3, 1953, pp. 310–5.

'Some reflections on the biblical material in the Manual of Discipline', *Studia Theologica* 9, 1955, pp. 40–66.

N. WIEDER, 'The Habakkuk Scroll and the Targum', JJS 4, 1953, pp. 14–18.

'"The Law Interpreter" of the sect of the Dead Sea Scrolls: the Second Moses', JJS 4, 1953, pp. 158–75.

'The term *QṢ* in the Dead Sea Scrolls and in Hebrew Liturgical Poetry', JJS 5, 1954, pp. 22–31.

'The Doctrine of the Two Messiahs among the Karaites', JJS 6, 1955, pp. 14–25.

E. WIESENBERG, 'Chronological Data in the Zadokite Fragments', VT 5, 1955, pp. 284–308.

H. WILDBERGER, 'Die "Sektenrolle" vom Toten Meer, *Evangelische Theologie* 1953, pp. 25–43.

'Der Dualismus in den Qumrânschriften', *Asiatische Studien*, 1954, pp. 163–77.

E. WILSON, *The Scrolls from the Dead Sea*, 1955.

P. WINTER, 'Notes on Wieder's Observations on the *DWRŠ HTWRH* in the Book of the New Covenanters of Damascus', JQR 45, 1954–5, pp. 39–47.

'Ben Sira and the Teaching of the Two Ways', VT 5, 1955, pp. 315–8.
A. S. van der Woude, see F. A. W. van't Land.
Y. Yadin, 'A Note on DSD IV 20', JBL 74, 1955, pp. 40–43.
The Scroll of the War of the Sons of Light against the Sons of Darkness (in Hebrew), Bialik Institute, Jerusalem, 1956.

GENERAL INDEX

BIBLICAL INDEX